D0114334

The U.S. Intelligence Community

The
U. S. Intelligence Community:

Foreign Policy and Domestic Activities

LYMAN B. KIRKPATRICK, JR.

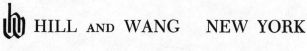 HILL AND WANG   NEW YORK

A division of Farrar, Straus and Giroux

Copyright © 1973 by LYMAN B. KIRKPATRICK, JR.

First printing, 1973

ISBN 0-8090-9501-7

Library of Congress catalog card number: 73-75184

Printed in the United States of America

Published simultaneously in Canada by

Doubleday Canada Ltd., Toronto

DESIGNED BY RONALD FARBER

For Rita

Contents

Preface

One of the great strengths of our American society, and one that assures both hope and confidence in the future, is the guarantee of freedom of speech and of the press by the Constitution of the United States. Perhaps nothing is more fundamental to our system than our right to speak out in criticism of our institutions. There are those who abuse this privilege for reasons of personal pique, political gain, or profit, and only time and the inevitable emergence of the truth can set the record straight.

In a period when so much nonsense is written about the Central Intelligence Agency and the intelligence community of the United States, it seems to me important to put before the public a book that sets the record straight. I completed my career in government eight years ago and have no desire to serve again except in case of emergency. I have no ax to grind, no personal pique, and no political ambitions: I have found academic life rewarding. Furthermore, one way to make money with a book is to write a sensational muckraker with all sorts of innuendos and hidden implications. This book, on the other hand, is a sober appraisal of the intelligence community. It is neither a defense nor a whitewash but an evaluation of the U.S. effort as I see it.

My main purpose here has been to discuss the intelligence community, but it should be understood by the

reader that other issues will be touched upon: the matter
of executive privilege; the relations between the Congress, the President, and the federal judiciary; and the
matter of the power of the federal bureaucracy, a dull
topic perhaps, but central to our contemporary political
life. And always present are the greater issues of international war and peace, and domestic tranquillity. It is not
grandiose to say that the agencies comprising the intelligence community play an important role in all of these issues.

Nearly twenty-three years in the intelligence services
of the United States—the Office of Strategic Services, the
U.S. Army, and the Central Intelligence Agency, almost
half of which were spent at the top echelon of CIA as Inspector General and Executive Director-Comptroller—
may have left me with impressions and convictions that
might be biased, but it should be noted that at this level I
was in a position to see both the best and the worst.

I imposed on many friends to read the manuscript in
draft, several of whom never served in intelligence. The
readers had only one thing in common: my respect for
their wisdom and judgment. I appreciate their taking the
time, and value their comments. These include my colleagues in the Political Science Department at Brown
University, Professors Elmer Cornwell and Erwin Har-
grove, and my assistant, Harry Latimer (shortly to add a
Ph.D. in Political Science to his accomplishments in the
Army). My friend for many years, Barnaby Conrad
Keeney, former president of Brown and now president of
Claremont Graduate College, made his usual trenchant
comments. Lieutenant Generals Clovis Byers (U.S.A.,
Ret.), Robert Breitweiser (U.S.A.F., Ret.), and Vice
Admiral Rufus Taylor (U.S.N., Ret.) enlightened me on
several points, and former Ambassador Foy Kohler, now
at the University of Miami, took time off from his own

writings to suggest some corrections, as did Hugh McKean, Chancellor of Rollins College. My neighbor Aram Jarret gave me added insight, as did my sister and brother-in-law, Helen and Robbins Milbank. My son, Lyman B. III, an officer in the regular Army, made detailed and penetrating comments.

I am indebted to the Carthage Foundation of Pittsburgh, Pennsylvania, for a grant which enabled me to have two research assistants, Robert John Turner, a graduate student at Brown University, and Kevin McEnery, an undergraduate, who assisted in collecting books and periodicals and checking details. The grant also provided for assistance in reproducing the manuscript.

My special thanks go to Walter Pforzheimer, who possesses perhaps the best private collection of intelligence literature in the world, for helping out in many areas. I am indebted to Tom Lewis, my editor at Hill and Wang, who first suggested the book and then made innumerable valuable comments.

My wife Rita was once again a patient and painstaking critic; she also typed the drafts and put up with my idiosyncrasies.

Having said all that, what I have written is what I believe to be the truth.

Lyman B. Kirkpatrick, Jr.

Anawan Cliffs
Narragansett, Rhode Island
April 1973

The U.S. Intelligence Community

1

The Intelligence Community

The phrase "the intelligence community" has been used to describe part of the U.S. government only in the last decade or so. Indeed, it was only during the same period that the American public became aware that something called "intelligence" was a vital element in the decision-making process of their government and that it was something more than stolen documents or information produced by spies.

Spies, informants, and those willing to steal documents are still an important part of any intelligence-collection system. Colonel Oleg Penkovsky of the Soviet State Scientific Committee produced valuable information for the Central Intelligence Agency in the 1960's. Neverthe-less, in modern times, U-2 aircraft, photographic satel-lites, and communications intelligence ships such as the *Pueblo* and *Liberty* tend to overshadow the role of the human agent. And the needs of the top policy-makers for accurate, detailed, and comprehensive knowledge of world developments have introduced vast numbers of researchers, analysts, and estimators supported by acres of computers into the intelligence process.

Before looking at the "community," a grounding in what constitutes intelligence is appropriate. Intelligence in modern terminology is a compilation and distillation of the total knowledge on any given area or subject.[1]

[1] See especially Part One, "Intelligence Is Knowledge," of Sherman Kent's

Intelligence must have a historical base. Russia has been
expansionist since the days of Peter the Great. Switzerland has followed a tradition of neutrality. Japan is
strongly influenced by its geography as an island nation.
The new nations of Africa exhibit some of the attributes
of the powers that once held them as colonies. Such
background knowledge is important for the analysis of
current information. Intelligence analysts must be deeply
versed in the history of their subject. A simple knowledge
of events is not sufficient. There must be an understanding of why nations take certain actions, why men make
specific decisions.

Added cumulatively to a historical background, the
information that creates intelligence comes from many
sources: some secret and sinister, most overtly available
and prosaic.

The traditional symbol of intelligence and mythical
purveyor of all information is the spy—the espionage
agent assigned to obtain the secrets of another power.
Although it is the most romantic of all sources of
intelligence, espionage has limitations not always accurately portrayed by the recorders of such activities. Few
spies of any note survive to write their memoirs, and
governments seldom make available documents on their
espionage operations. It is quite conceivable that in
earlier times an espionage agent could obtain all the
necessary information about the strength and plans of a
nation by developing contacts in an imperial court or
among the leaders of a republic. With the increasing
complexity of society and the sizable organizations
required to manage government, the economy, or the
technology, it is most unlikely that any one agent could
obtain more than a small portion of the secrets of a major

excellent book *Strategic Intelligence* (Princeton, N.J.: Princeton University
Press, 1949, 1966).

nation. Not even a president, king, or first secretary would possess more than general knowledge.

This is well illustrated by the case of Colonel Penkovsky, who provided more than five thousand top-secret documents during his brief but terminal career as a spy. While the U.S. government did not make public Penkovsky's reports, it can be assumed that he was able to obtain only those documents that the State Scientific Committee received to accomplish its task, and not the entire encyclopedia of secrets of the Soviet Union. This is not to demean the exceptionally valuable material produced by Penkovsky but to emphasize that in modern times a spy can produce only that information to which he has access under normal conditions. Thus no American in the Soviet Union could ever have reached the material to which Penkovsky had access: only a Russian could—and one with clearance to see top-secret material.

In simplest terms, in modern times a spy is almost invariably a citizen of the country against which the espionage is being committed; one who has access to some of the innermost secrets of his government, and one who for some reason is willing to commit treason and betray his nation to a foreign power.

The motives of a person who commits treason are never easy to explain.[2] Ideology, greed, and ambition all play a role. In most countries the penalty for espionage is death, and the rewards to the individual are remarkably small considering the risk. However, it is probable that espionage will continue to be a source of intelligence information as long as governments have secrets.

The necessity for spies is apparent. There is informa-

---

[2] See Rebecca West, *The New Meaning of Treason* (New York: Viking Press, 1964).

tion only a human agent can obtain, information rarely
put in documents or on communications channels: what
government leaders intend to do under given circumstances. Most modern and sophisticated governments
have contingency plans for the future, but frequently
these are changed when the time for action arrives. In
times of emergency or crisis, every precaution for security is observed. A nation's course of action is then known
by a few top leaders and is communicated by word of
mouth. Only an agent in the proper place is likely to
obtain such information.

Adolf Hitler was well aware of this principle when he
launched the German offensive through the Ardennes
Forest in December 1944. Only the most senior officers
were aware of the plan for the attack until just a few
hours before it was launched, and they had to sign a
special secrecy agreement which advised them they
could be executed if there was a leak. Unfortunately,
none of these German officers worked for U.S. intelligence and the attack caught the Americans by surprise.[3]

Over the long haul, however, spies are most valuable
when they can obtain or copy official documents. Intelligence organizations are highly skeptical of the information their agents produce and regard reports of conversations or information obtained through subagents as less
valuable than photographs of official documents. Even
photographs of documents are viewed with reserve as
possible forgeries or "plants." Not until an agent's
product has been checked against other sources or has
proven reliable over a period of time is it accepted as
accurate, and even then with some reservation, especially
when new or unusual developments are reported.

[3] For an analysis of the intelligence failure, see Chapter 6, "The Bulge in the
Ardennes: Hitler's Last Threat, Dec. 16, 1944," in Lyman B. Kirkpatrick, Jr.,
Captains without Eyes: Intelligence Failures in World War II (New York:
Macmillan, 1969). The bibliography of that chapter gives further references.

It was obvious that Joseph Stalin apparently had little faith in the Russian intelligence services prior to the German attack on the Soviet Union in June 1941. Intelligence nets based in Switzerland and in Japan warned him of Hitler's plans, including the exact date of the offensive. Stalin ignored this information, as well as warnings from the Americans and British.

A second source of intelligence, nearly as ancient as the espionage agent, is the interception of communications. The first interception of communications probably occurred before ancient man started to inscribe messages on clay tablets, when some courier, given an oral dispatch, was waylaid and had the information beaten out of him. Once man started to communicate in writing, the stealing of documents from messengers became a practice of intelligence services. When carrier pigeons came into use as a method of communications, interception by falcon, slingshot, arrow, and gun became the practice. Smoke signals, semaphores, and flashing lights were used to communicate—and were intercepted. The mails, telegraph, telephone, and finally radio, in turn, became the objects of interception. Even lip-reading has been used.

By the 1970's electronic transmissions of every type were intercepted. The high-speed radio transmissions of a nation communicating with its missions abroad were a prime target. Military signals were listened to with particular interest. The transmitters in missiles and satellites sending messages to the planet earth and the messages from ground stations directing the vehicles were intercepted when possible. Commercial telegraphic traffic evoked occasional interest. The insatiable maw of the intelligence community analyzed every communication of any conceivable interest, anxious to gain clues to information on the strengths or intentions of other nations.

Interception was not always enlightening. Even as the first highwayman was stealing the other fellow's documents, men were starting to conceal the true meaning of their messages. It started with simple, previously arranged innocent-text messages: "The sun is red at dawn" meant "We will attack on Thursday." [4] Ciphers (substitution or transposition of letters to hide meaning), codes (chosen words, letters, or symbols assigned definite meanings), and invisible writing were soon added to the arsenal to defend communications against prying. As a nation's requirements to communicate grew from cryptic instructions and reports to complicated commands covering every contingency and comprehensive analyses of political developments, simple codes and ciphers laboriously processed by hand no longer sufficed, increasingly complex machines were developed to encode messages automatically.

Thus, while great volumes of messages are intercepted, the number that can be read and understood has been progressively declining over the years. Generally, it is the careless communicator or the casual government that lets secrets slip. However, even in the absence of reading the other nation's communications, some valuable information can be gleaned through such techniques as traffic analysis; for example, the frequency of messages between specific points, volume at given periods of time, etc.[5]

Communications intelligence was primarily responsible

---

[4] Even the age of supersophistication in communications has not rendered the innocent-text message obsolete. In December 1941 the Japanese broadcast "East wind rain" in clear text to warn its missions overseas that war was imminent.

[5] The best history of secret communications, including a description of modern techniques, is David Kahn, *The Codebreakers* (New York: Macmillan, 1967).

for enabling the U.S. Navy to have its forces in the right place at the right time in the battle of Midway, June 4, 1942. Admiral Yamamoto launched an attack on the Aleutians to lure the Americans north while he captured Midway, planning with his overwhelming superiority (11 battleships, 5 carriers, 16 cruisers, and 49 destroyers versus no battleships, 3 carriers, 8 cruisers, and 14 destroyers) to drive the U.S. Navy from the Pacific. Instead, as a result of the United States having solved the Japanese-fleet cryptographic system, four of the Imperial Navy's carriers were sunk (the Americans lost the *Yorktown*) and Yamamoto withdrew.

A third source of intelligence which could possibly be included as communications but deserves a separate listing is audio surveillance. This goes far beyond tapping telephone lines and now includes a massive array of technical devices. No mission located on foreign soil can consider itself immune from audio surveillance. The amazing age of electronics has produced minute microphones and transmitters that can be surreptitiously placed in books, pictures, or drapes; in table legs, radiators, and light fixtures; behind the lapel of a suit coat; or wherever an imaginative agent can conceal them—to send every word or sound to a nearby listening post. What is necessary for this type of intelligence collection is access to the target room for placing the device and a listening post sufficiently nearby to receive from the tiny transmitter. If a lapel microphone is used, a wire to a small recorder or pocket transmitter is used. Even direct access is no longer always needed, as beams have been developed that can be directed at a window from a distance to pick up conversations in the room behind.

American security and counterintelligence officers have discovered more than once that the United States has been on the receiving end of audio surveillance in its embassy in Moscow. In the 1950's, it was discovered that the Russians had implanted a passive resonant cavity microphone in the Great Seal of the United States. This device, which resembled a doll's tiny frying pan, reflected an electric beam focused on it from a nearby "listening post," transmitting what was being said in the room. A few years later, scores of microphones were uncovered in the walls of the embassy when a technical inspection revealed a few "bugs," which led to ripping out all the plaster. In short, there was little, if anything, said or done in the U.S. embassy in Moscow during that time except under the most secure conditions that was not known to the Russians.

A fourth source of information, one that has burgeoned as man has conquered space, is photographic intelligence. Not long after the invention of the camera, it became possible to photograph documents, one of the principal occupations of the well-placed espionage agent. It was war, both hot and cold, that moved the camera from a secondary to a primary source of intelligence. In the First World War men leaned over the sides of airplanes to photograph enemy trenches and installations. In the Second World War photographic reconnaissance had advanced to a stage where specially equipped aircraft, flying at ten to fifteen thousand feet over enemy territory, produced hundreds of feet of film to be scanned intensively by trained photo-interpreters. Less than a decade after the end of that war, photographic reconnaissance made another giant stride forward when U-2 aircraft photographed targets from great altitudes and produced better pictures than those taken from a fraction of that altitude a few years earlier. The U-2 proved to be a source of intelligence on Russian industrial and military developments of inestimable value to the United States.

By the time the U-2's service in Russia was terminated by a missile over Sverdlovsk on May 1, 1960, the photographic satellite was in operation, filming the earth from a distance of one hundred miles or more with sufficient quality to produce excellent information.

Even before the end of the U-2's career was in sight, a new reconnaissance aircraft was under construction—one that could fly much higher and faster than the U-2. With the photographic satellite already in use, and less offensive to national sovereignty, this aircraft, variously known as the A-11 and the SR-71, was not used operationally until the war in Vietnam.

While airborne cameras cannot reproduce government documents or penetrate the minds of men, in the last third of the twentieth century it is feasible that the key areas of the earth's surface can be kept under continual visual surveillance.

The fifth source of information available to the intelligence community is government reporting. A quick look at the State Department publication listing U.S. missions abroad gives an order of magnitude: 124 embassies, 68 consulates-general, and 45 consulates in 247 different locations. Great numbers of reports are dispatched to Washington each day containing information of interest to the United States. None of it is intelligence per se, but much of it is of value in the intelligence process.

The principal departments and agencies of the U.S. government openly represented in its missions abroad give an indication of the types of reports forwarded to Washington:

—The Foreign Service is the diplomatic representative primarily charged with intergovernmental negotiations, continually reporting in this area and on all matters affecting relations of foreign countries with the United States; occasionally, a seemingly inconsequential social item may provide a valuable aid to the intelligence analysts: a rare smile or cordial handshake by a party secretary in a Communist country may indicate an imminent change in policy.

—The Consular Service is charged with the development of commercial relations and produces a large volume of economic information. The great importance of world trade makes this an important ingredient in the intelligence community.

—Defense Department personnel in the offices of the service attachés are accredited to the local military services with which they maintain liaison. Sometimes acute observation in this type of liaison can produce valuable intelligence. In 1941 a U.S. Army attaché in Berlin noticed that an officer of the German High Command had replaced the wall maps of Western Europe with those of the Soviet Union and correctly forecast the attack on Russia.

—The United States Information Agency (USIA) deals with the local media, distributes information about America, and operates libraries, and is also acutely aware of public opinion in each country. Reports from the USIA's Public Affairs Officer in the field supplement those of the diplomatic corps on attitudes toward the United States, which in turn helps determine American policy.

—The Agency for International Development (AID) provides financial, technical, and material assistance, including a public-safety program for the training and equipping of the police forces. The details that are accumulated by AID in assessing developmental assistance projects are studied by the economic analysts of the intelligence community.

—Treasury Department representatives are concerned with economic reporting. The importance of the information from the Treasury representatives is reflected in the addition of that department to the United States Intelligence Board (USIB) in November 1971.

One could enlarge this list to include at one time or another, in one place or another, practically every department or agency of the government. It should be noted that most of the official reports from the departments and agencies listed above are either provided by or made available with the knowledge of the host government. This type of reporting is the essence of modern international relations.

There are many examples of vital information received by the U.S. government from official reporting—information which by itself constitutes intelligence of great importance. Ambassadors frequently are the first to receive advice of a nation's intentions. Summoned to the host nation's foreign office, they are informed of a specific and important change in that nation's attitude toward matters of interest to the United States. The mere manner of Foreign Office officials toward American representatives—cordiality or coldness—provides a clue for intelligence of possible developments. In October 1956 the U.S. Army attaché in Tel Aviv advised that the Israeli Army had mobilized and was going to attack Egypt through the Sinai. This vital intelligence report, taken with many other bits and pieces emanating from the area, some of them deliberate plants and fabrications to mislead the U.S. government, alerted the Watch Committee[6] of the intelligence community to the impending crisis. After many long sessions trying to sort fact from fabrication, the Watch Committee advised the President that they were convinced that Israel was going

---

[6] The Watch Committee is chaired by an Assistant Director of Central Intelligence and its membership consists of representatives of all the intelligence agencies.

to attack Egypt. This enabled President Eisenhower to remonstrate with the British, French, and Israeli governments in an effort to prevent that war.

Ironically, not only did the intelligence agencies never get credit for this excellent work but they were publicly denounced by Congressmen, commentators, and others for the fact that the United States was taken by surprise. Secretary of State John Foster Dulles had chosen to say that he had not been informed of the attack, meaning by the Israeli, British, or French governments, but it was assumed that he meant the intelligence system had failed. Congressman Mahon of Texas, visiting the CIA building shortly thereafter, passed the intelligence chiefs as they were leaving a meeting and made the comment: "Where were all those fellows when the Suez War started?"

The sixth source of information for the intelligence process is public information: books, official reports, scholarly journals, radio broadcasts, television, newspapers, and magazines. Public radio alone provides unique information. More than six million words spout forth from the radio transmitters of the world every twenty-four hours, and a trickle from this vast flow provides new information. The Foreign Broadcast Information Service, an office of the CIA, has a worldwide monitoring service to listen to what is being said and to record and publish what seems noteworthy. Occasionally, new and valuable information comes from this source. The Soviet Union first revealed that it planned to resume nuclear testing in the atmosphere in 1955 in an internal news dispatch which was heard by the Western monitoring services.

Newspapers and periodicals are scanned for any information that might add to the knowledge of the intelligence services. Even more important are the many journals—scientific, technical, economic, medical. These sources of intelligence produce millions of items of information each year—information that must be analyzed, weighed against all other knowledge of the same subject, and discarded, if of no use, or stored to be retrieved when needed. Such a process requires a considerable staff: information specialists, librarians, computer programmers, analysts, technicians, researchers, area experts, and others. The sheer number of people, if nothing else, makes today's intelligence community far different from anything that preceded it.

The processing of intelligence reports must be timely, with meticulous attention given to detail and the reliability of the source. The collection of accurate information is difficult in itself, and the continuing battle of intelligence services adds to the difficulty. There are always "paper mills" to be contended with: individuals or groups who sell allegedly secret reports to any and all intelligence services. The Soviet intelligence services paid rather substantial sums in Stockholm for a series of reports concocted by an imaginative journalist. American intelligence services also have bought reports written by enterprising émigrés. Fabrications also emanate from official services in deliberate deception programs designed to mislead the opposing intelligence organization. The frauds are not confined to reports allegedly from agents on-the-spot but include forgeries of official documents, touched-up photographs, radio messages giving inaccurate information, and even planted press reports. The limits in this undercover war are imposed only by man's imagination and ingenuity, or an inhibited bureaucracy.[7]

With such possibilities of error, a first step in the

[7] See the testimony of former Director of Central Intelligence Richard Helms before the subcommittee to investigate the administration of the Internal Security Act of the Committee on the Judiciary, U.S. Senate, June 2, 1961 (Washington: Government Printing Office).

intelligence process is an evaluation of the source at the place of collection. Reports from the diplomatic corps usually contain full details on the "what, where, when, why, and how" so necessary for the analyst, many days later and thousands of miles away, properly to weigh the importance of the information. "I saw the Foreign Minister today at his request. We lunched together alone at his residence and he gave me a full run-down on his government's views of the deepening regional crisis and the threat from Ruritania. I felt he was being unusually candid. He said . . ." Photographs taken from the air or on the surface must be captioned with the exact date and time, geographical coordinates or precise location, the light conditions, and a description of the subject. Communications intelligence reports should have the time, date, and place of transmission, identity of sender and recipient, method of transmission, and any other information, such as priority of message, that would assist the analyst.

Evaluating the reliability of a report from a clandestine agent or spy poses especially difficult problems. The agent is seldom, if ever, an American, although he may be working for a U.S. case officer. The agent is usually indigenous to the area where he or she operates and is recruited primarily because of access to the desired information. Thus the agent is not necessarily skilled in observation, reporting, or communications. It will be the responsibility of the case officer to train the agent in these skills, as well as possible under the circumstances, and to evaluate the reports produced on the basis of an intimate knowledge of the agent's abilities. If the report is a copy of a government document, many questions must be answered, such as: How did the agent have access to such a document? Did he open a safe and photograph it? Did he have a subsource in the government who made it available? Might it be a "plant," deliberately placed for the agent to find it? (And this, of course, leads to the always present possibility that the agent might be a "double" working for the other side, too.) If the report is not the copy of a document, the questions must be equally searching: Did an authority give it to him? Did he attend the meeting where it was discussed? Did he overhear it in a bar? Is he an accurate reporter? inclined to exaggerate? Thus the report collected clandestinely should be forwarded on to Washington only with careful evaluations of the agent's capabilities and of the field officer's judgment of the accuracy of the information.

The handling of the "raw reports"—those that have not yet been weighed in relation to all other knowledge on the subject—is equally careful in Washington. Perhaps an appropriate analogy is to liken the process to a series of filters, with the volume of information moving upward toward the top of the intelligence system or laterally to other departments or agencies, the volume decreasing as it moves through the system. The headquarters of each collection agency in Washington screens the reports coming in from the field and may eliminate or delay some because of questions about the reliability of the source or the necessity to go back to the field for more details.

The first analysis of the substance of the report comes at the "desk" level in the consumer departments—State, Defense, Treasury, CIA—where each looks at all reports in their specialty. The State Department desk officer for country X generally will see all reports on political matters affecting that nation and perhaps on other subjects if the volume and his time permit. In Treasury, the X desk officers will examine all economic and financial reports. In CIA, the X desk may look at reports on all subjects, while in Defense the X desks in the

Defense Intelligence Agency and those of Army, Navy, and Air intelligence will concentrate on military matters of specific interest. Thus with hundreds of desk officers in Washington reviewing the daily flow of thousands of reports, the incoming intelligence gets prompt and effective action when warranted.

Actually, a very small number of raw reports reaches the policy level of the government after the review at desk level, and those that do are screened at several other levels on the way up. An exceptionally important report may be forwarded to the decision-making level by a special memorandum. The most usual method is for the report to be included in one of the daily intelligence summaries for the President, copies of which will go to the secretaries of State, Defense, Treasury, and the Joint Chiefs of Staff.

The great bulk of the raw reports become additional items in the files to be used when a study is prepared on "The Political Outlook in X," "Defense-Related Industry in X," "The Quality of the X Air Force." Such studies in turn become the basis for National Intelligence Estimates and Surveys. In summary, raw intelligence reports can reach the decision-makers in the government through special memoranda, daily intelligence digests, National Intelligence Estimates, and National Intelligence Surveys.

The method for producing the studies for the decision-makers is important, and measures are taken to insure that all the concerned intelligence agencies have the opportunity to contribute. Each agency produces reports under its own label, but those studies designated "National" generally constitute contributions from all members of the intelligence community produced under the guidance of the CIA.

The National Intelligence Surveys are classified encyclopedias of the world: compilations on everything from agriculture and atomic energy to military and industrial potential. The initial production of the surveys took many years, with contributions from the qualified departments and agencies. The surveys are updated periodically.

The National Intelligence Estimates (NIE) deal with current problems of vital interest: "The Prospects for Peace in the Middle East," "The Capabilities and Intentions of the Soviet Union: 1974–1979," "World Reaction to U.S. Trade Restrictions," "Possibilities for a General Agreement on Arms Limitation." These projections, tailored to the specific needs of the President and the principal policy-makers, also are products of the intelligence community drafted under the direction of the Board of National Estimates located in the Office of the Director of Central Intelligence. A task force is set up for each estimate consisting of representatives of the intelligence agencies and directed by a member of the Board of National Estimates. Each agency drafts that portion within its area of expertise: State on political matters, DIA or one of the services on military, CIA and Treasury on economic, etc. The staff of the board consolidates all submissions into a second draft. The "reps" then attempt to reach agreement with the board while keeping their own directors informed. The final version goes to the United States Intelligence Board where the directors try to work out differences. The Director of Central Intelligence makes the final decision, but the heads of the other agencies can disagree, explaining their dissent in a footnote. Thus the President gets a consolidated point of view from the intelligence community and also an indication of any strongly held dissents.

Inasmuch as all participants are working from the same base of information, disagreements mostly result from differing interpretations, varied projections, and attempts to anticipate the unseen and unknown. The most serious controversies have arisen over the Soviet missile force—its strength and purpose—most especially whether it is intended to have a first-strike capability or solely that of a massive deterrence.

With this background of the raw material of intelligence, let us look at the emergence of the intelligence community. The history of the use of intelligence by the U.S. government portrays a very erratic and inconsistent course. During the Revolutionary War, intelligence was an individual and almost personal matter on the part of the commander. James Thomas Flexner in his biography of George Washington describes him as his own master of intelligence.

> Washington's first large expenditures after his arrival in Cambridge had been $333.33 for someone "to go into the town of Boston to establish secret correspondence."
> Washington stationed lookouts on all commanding heights; he urged skirmishes to capture prisoners who could be interrogated. "Leave no stone unturned, nor do not stick at any expense" to procure spies.
> He was endlessly busy directing spies, analyzing the information they brought in.[8]

The intelligence "estimates" of the time were prepared by Major General Benjamin Lincoln, the Secretary of War.[9]

Washington's interest in intelligence did not carry over to peacetime. The fledgling nation learned what it could

---

[8] James Thomas Flexner, *George Washington: In the American Revolution 1775–1783* (Boston: Little, Brown, 1968), pp. 44, 119, 204. Another study of spies in the Revolutionary War is John E. Bakeless, *Turncoats, Traitors and Heroes* (Philadelphia: Lippincott, 1959).

[9] Russell F. Weigley, *History of the United States Army* (New York: Macmillan, 1967), p. 49.

about potential enemies from friends or the local efforts of individual officials, but the official creation of a national intelligence system was a century and a half away. Information from abroad came primarily from diplomats or military personnel on foreign assignment. When the American military forces found themselves at war, an intelligence department was manned, only to be drastically reduced in size or disbanded at the cessation of hostilities. During the Mexican War it was the Inspector General of the expeditionary force who organized the spies, and after the war the Secretary of War, Jefferson Davis, was reluctant to reimburse General Scott for the secret-service activities because the latter refused to divulge any details.[10] At the start of the First World War, only two officers and two clerks in the War Department had been concerned with the gathering of intelligence. In August 1918 the Chief of Staff, General Peyton C. March, created four main General Staff divisions: Operations; Military Intelligence; Purchase, Storage, and Traffic; and War Plans. The number of people in intelligence rose to 282 officers, 29 enlisted personnel, and 949 civilians.[11] In 1921 General Pershing modified the staff in Washington slightly after the pattern of his Allied Expeditionary Force (AEF), and the Military Intelligence Division became known also as G-2. The evolution of the intelligence staffs in Washington was paralleled by the development of a system of military attachés assigned to U.S. embassies abroad. Congress passed a law authorizing military and naval attachés on September 22, 1888. The first five were assigned the following year to Berlin, Paris, London, Vienna, and St. Petersburg. Within the next five years, Rome, Brussels,

[10] *Ibid.*, pp. 182 and 194.
[11] *Ibid.*, pp. 379–80.

Madrid, Tokyo, and Mexico City were added. For many years the number was limited, and in some cases attachés were temporarily assigned during periods of international crisis.[12]

Fortunately, one legacy from the First World War was an interest in maintaining a capability in the communications intelligence which had proved of such value to the Allies. The State and War Departments combined in a joint venture known as "The American Black Chamber," which was to be an important source of communications intelligence until 1929.[13] The State Department, imbued with a philosophy that diplomacy should be open and aboveboard, disbanded its cryptographic bureau; legend has it that the then Secretary of State Henry Stimson explained the move with the comment: "Gentlemen do not read each other's mail." The Army and Navy, perhaps less convinced of the gentlemanly quality of the rest of the world, continued their cryptographic work, which proved of incalculable value in the war with Japan.

The cryptographers were able to break the so-called Purple Code of the Japanese, which was used to transmit top-secret diplomatic and military messages between Tokyo and its representatives abroad during the period prior to the attack on Pearl Harbor. As a consequence, senior American officials in Washington were reading the instructions that the Japanese Foreign Ministry was sending to its negotiators in Washington almost as soon as the addressees could read them. These instructions included the lengthy fourteen-part message received on

[12] Alfred Vagts, *The Military Attaché* (Princeton, N.J.: Princeton University Press, 1967), p. 33.
[13] The classic description of this organization is by its talented founder, Herbert O. Yardley, *The American Black Chamber* (Indianapolis: Bobbs-Merrill, 1931).

December 6, 1941, which told the Japanese ambassadors to break off negotiations and which, in turn, resulted in a warning sent from U.S. officials in Washington to the military forces in Hawaii to be prepared for a possible attack; this was being delivered by a Western Union messenger on bicycle at the moment Japanese bombers were attacking the fleet at Pearl Harbor.

During the Second World War a new organization was created in Washington, the Office of Strategic Services (OSS). The OSS was the brainchild of William J. Donovan, a New York lawyer who had commanded the "Fighting 69th" Regiment in the first war and been awarded the Medal of Honor. Donovan persuaded President Roosevelt that the United States needed a special organization to conduct secret intelligence activities, engage in such special operations as establishing paramilitary units behind enemy lines, wage psychological warfare with black propaganda (false information purporting to come from the enemy), and other means to undermine the German and Japanese morale, and do research in depth on subjects of strategic interest.

At the conclusion of the Second World War, the OSS was disbanded, but personnel of three of its branches were kept on duty and incorporated into the new federal intelligence structure. The Research and Analysis Branch was assigned as a unit to the State Department. The Counterintelligence[14] and Secret Intelligence Branches were temporarily assigned to the War Department, later to be transferred to the Central Intelligence Group (CIG) when it came into being in 1946.[15]

[14] This should not be confused with the Counterintelligence Corps, or CIC, of the Army. The OSS effort was more in the area of counterespionage.

[15] For further details on the OSS, see Corey Ford, *Donovan of O.S.S.* (Boston: Little, Brown, 1970), and R. Harris Smith, *O.S.S.: The Secret History of America's First Central Intelligence Agency* (Berkeley, Calif.: University of California Press, 1972).

Within the State Department there was controversy as to whether the intelligence responsibility should reside in the area bureaus or maintain a separate identity. Shortly after the OSS Research and Analysis Branch was transferred to State, Secretary James Byrnes assigned the research and intelligence specialists to the various "desks." In February 1947 Secretary of State George C. Marshall centralized the intelligence function into the Office of Intelligence Research. One of the principles behind this reorganization was to provide an analysis of information independent of the area "desks" where recommendations for policy originate.

The military intelligence services, having expanded to unprecedented size during the Second World War, were determined to maintain some organizations of consequence during peacetime. While each suffered drastic reductions during the precipitous demobilization after 1945, the Navy, Army, and Army Air Forces (to become the United States Air Force) all managed to preserve respectable intelligence establishments which became members of the new postwar structure.

On January 22, 1946, the first step was taken toward the creation of the system that is now popularly called "the intelligence community." President Truman issued an Executive Letter establishing the Central Intelligence Group, the forerunner of the Central Intelligence Agency, and creating a National Intelligence Authority (NIA) composed of the Secretaries of State, War, and Navy and a personal representative of the President. In eighteen months the CIG became the nucleus of the CIA, and the functions of the NIA were taken over by the National Security Council (NSC). Both of the new organizations were established by the National Security Act of 1947.

It is interesting to note that in his memoirs President

Truman, speaking of this legislation, says, "The other valuable agencies created by the Act were a Central Intelligence Agency under the Security Council, to correlate and evaluate intelligence activities and data. . . ." The phrasing is significant. It is obvious from his recollections that President Truman placed great stress on the necessity for a coordinated system under centralized direction. He notes that not much attention had been paid to the creation of any centralized intelligence organization in the government, and recalls that it was Fleet Admiral William D. Leahy, his military adviser, who told him about a plan for such an organization prepared during the Second World War by OSS Director Major General William J. Donovan and submitted in 1944 to President Roosevelt and the Joint Chiefs of Staff.

Between Donovan's original proposal in 1944 and the establishment of the CIA in 1947, considerable discussion and controversy had been generated by the problems of establishing a permanent peacetime intelligence system. There was agreement on only one major issue: no department, bureau, or agency would willingly surrender its right to collect, evaluate, and disseminate that intelligence that it considered important to its own needs. The Army and the Navy were in favor of centralized direction, subject to the above qualification. Secretary of State James Byrnes proposed that the responsibility for all intelligence be placed in the State Department under his direction. Other departments had different views.

The passage of the National Security Act in 1947 neither stilled the jurisdictional controversies nor brought into being a strong centralized organization. It did provide the legislative authority for the creation of such a system.

Some portions of the 1947 act[16] seem precise in intent.

[16] 61 Stat. 495, 50 U.S.C. 401.

The CIA provisions are under "Title I—Coordination for National Security." The title is a clear indication of intent: a coordinated system under central direction. The first section, 102 (a) reads, in part: "There is hereby established under the National Security Council a Central Intelligence Agency with a Director of Central Intelligence who shall be the head thereof. . . ." The centralized principle is again emphasized in the title of the Director "of Central Intelligence." Subparagraph (d) of this same section further expands on this: "For the purpose of coordinating the intelligence activities of the several Government departments and agencies in the interest of national security, it shall be the duty of the Agency, under the direction of the National Security Council—

"(1) To advise . . . in matters concerning such intelligence activities . . .

"(2) to make recommendations . . . for coordination . . .

"(3) to correlate and evaluate intelligence . . . using where appropriate existing agencies and facilities."

The law goes on to require that other departments and agencies provide intelligence to the Director of Central Intelligence and open their files for his inspection upon request. Perhaps the drafters of the statute did not foresee the way in which the intelligence community would develop and therefore did not specify in greater detail the methods for coordination.

Certainly the authors of the law would have had difficulty in predicting that in its first quarter-century the newly created intelligence system would be faced with U.S. participation in two major wars, scores of other conflicts and armed insurgencies in which the United States had specific interests, a nation explosion that doubled the number of independent states in the world, an arms race, and the technological revolution. In any event, the broad provisions of the law gave necessary authority for the evolution of a centralized system.

Other measures in the law also prescribed the method by which the system would develop. One clearly ensured that the Federal Bureau of Investigation (FBI) would continue to be the principal organization responsible for internal security. It reads: "Provided. That the Agency (CIA) shall have no police, subpoena, law-enforcement powers, or internal security functions."

The established intelligence services were protected with the provision: "*Provided further,* That the departments and other agencies of the Government shall continue to collect, evaluate, correlate and disseminate departmental intelligence."

Very specific powers were given to the DCI regarding the security of the intelligence community: ". . . The Director of Central Intelligence shall be responsible for protecting intelligence sources and methods from unauthorized disclosure."

And, finally, the National Security Act wisely included omnibus clauses by which the National Security Council (or the President) could use the CIA to assist in the implementation of foreign policy: "Section 102 (d) (4) to perform . . . such services of common concern as the National Security Council determines can be more efficiently accomplished centrally; (5) to perform such other duties related to intelligence affecting the national security as the National Security Council may from time to time direct." It does not require a constitutional lawyer to recognize the tremendous power these clauses give the President to use the CIA as a vehicle for covert political warfare. The phrases "services of common concern" and "such other duties related to intelligence affecting the national security" have been interpreted as

legal authority for such diverse activities as running a
registry of biographical intelligence on behalf of the
intelligence community, building and operating U-2
aircraft for photo-reconnaissance, and attempting to
overthrow Fidel Castro at the Bay of Pigs.

One can reflect that it might have been better if the
U.S. intelligence community had been able to develop
under more tranquil world conditions than those following the passage of the 1947 act; but this can be
countered with the argument that the development of a
coordinated and centralized system might have been
even more difficult without the pressures to get results
which often forced concessions on jurisdictional issues
and retreat from parochial positions.

The period from 1947 to 1950 could be described as
either post–Second World War or the start of the Cold
War. As postwar, it was a time when the U.S military
services were demobilizing at a rate that General George
C. Marshall described as a "rout." Demobilization included the intelligence staffs. This forced reduction of
military intelligence responsibilities eased the creation of
centralized services: faced with having functions abol-
ished or being transferred to the CIA, the Army and the
Navy chose the latter.

With the withdrawal of the armed forces from overseas, there was only limited interest by these organizations in engaging in intelligence operations. Both the
Army and the Navy had developed organizations for
handling captured documents. These went to the CIA to
become the nucleus of a foreign documents office. The
Federal Communications Commission monitored foreign
broadcasts during the Second World War but sought to
disestablish the practice at the end of hostilities. Wiser
heads prevailed and the wartime organization was main-

tained, transferred briefly to the War Department and then to the Central Intelligence Group.

During this period before 1950, the CIA still was working out organizational details. Its fairly substantial cadre of personnel who had started their intelligence careers in the wartime OSS, the FBI, or the military services was readjusting to peacetime conditions. The Intelligence Advisory Committee (the chiefs of the intelligence services) was having the difficulties one would expect from a body composed of equals with limited precedents and experience in centralized or coordinated activities.

The communications intelligence services of the armed forces succeeded in maintaining respectable strength; certainly not as large as they wished, but still effective. Most of those in the military service who were aware of the breaking of the Japanese Purple Code were certain of the value of such services. There was, however, pressure for unification of the effort. In 1949 the Defense Department created an Armed Forces Security Agency. On November 4, 1952, this became the National Security Agency (NSA), the centralized communications security and intelligence component reporting directly to the Defense Department. The three military services kept their own agencies, which became the collecting and processing organizations under NSA's direction.

The importance of communications intelligence in wartime was illustrated by the value to the U.S. Navy of the intercepted Japanese messages in the battle of Midway. That it is a major area of activity in peacetime is indicated by the intense interest of the Soviet Union in NSA personnel: on September 6, 1960, two former employees, William Martin and Bernon Mitchell, were given the theater of the Hall of Journalists in Moscow to

COMMUNICATIONS INTELLIGENCE (Simplified)*

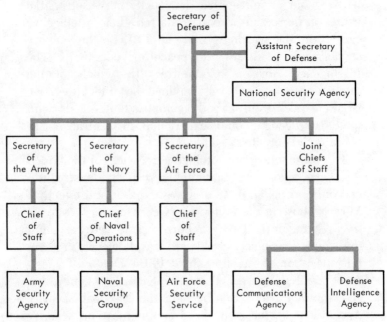

* Only the pertinent agencies are included
and certain intermediary echelons are excluded.

Source: Rita Kirkpatrick

stage a press conference to describe U.S. successes in communications intelligence; on July 23, 1963, *Izvestia* published a letter from another ex-employee; at about the same time, Sergeant Jack Dunlap, an Army man assigned to NSA, committed suicide when a security investigation revealed he had been selling classified documents to the Russians. The revelations in these cases, perhaps surprising to some Americans, illustrate the magnitude of the modern communications intelligence effort: extensive interception, cryptoanalysis, acquisition of code books and information about encryption techniques, and traffic analysis.

The outbreak of the Korean War in June 1950 opened a new era in intelligence development, one of rapid expansion in an effort to meet the demands on the part of military commanders and policy-makers for information and for mounting "intelligence-related" activities. The military intelligence services were rebuilt to support the expanded forces. Despite the most intense efforts on the part of the intelligence services, many in Washington and in overseas units were shocked and disappointed that the CIA and other agencies had not become omniscient in the brief period of postwar existence.

The year 1950 saw another major development in the U.S. intelligence community. Lieutenant General Walter Bedell Smith (shortly thereafter to receive his fourth star) became the Director of Central Intelligence. As Secretary of the General Staff to General George C. Marshall in the Pentagon, as Chief of Staff to General Dwight D. Eisenhower in Europe, as Ambassador to Russia, as Commanding General of the First U.S. Army, Smith had diplomatic and military experience. He had lived with centralization, coordination, and command. He had the rank and the personality to do the job, and,

perhaps most important of all, he had the strong backing
of President Harry S. Truman.

- Under the persistent prodding of General Smith, the
intelligence community moved toward coordination and
centralization. He was impatient with jurisdictional arguments, whether within the CIA or among the services.
His attitude was that there was more than enough work
for everybody. He had the authority and used it.

Within the CIA he reorganized the operational arm,
established new guidelines for interagency cooperation,
and established a support arm to provide the personnel,
training, communications, logistics, and security so necessary in intelligence activities. He separated research from
the estimating process and proposed a division of research responsibilities among the intelligence agencies.
The Intelligence Advisory Committee gained stature as
the governing body of the community.

Perhaps no action more typified the style and personality of General Smith than the organization of the
operational offices of the CIA. The agency had inherited
its foreign intelligence and counterintelligence offices
from the OSS, and in the five years since the Second
World War these had been consolidated, reorganized,
and reoriented to peacetime conditions. By 1948 another
office had been added to engage in covert operations or
political warfare. The new office was in, but not of, the
CIA. It took its directives from a State-Defense committee, not the DCI. One of Smith's first actions on
becoming director in October 1950 was to announce that
he would issue the orders to this office. He later directed
that the two offices (foreign intelligence and covert
operations) be merged and that the deputy director
concerned and the two assistant directors in charge of
those offices work out the details. As one of the assistant
directors, I participated in what were extended and
exhaustive negotiations. In the summer of 1952 Smith

finally accepted our proposals and called a meeting of all of the division and staff chiefs of the to-be-merged offices to announce the new organization. Although everyone present knew that the director was impatient to have the merger implemented, there were a couple who wanted to argue it. Smith gave them short shrift: his quick temper flared and he scathingly stopped the discussion, announced what was to take place, and stalked out. One of my colleagues leaned over and whispered, "My God, if he is that terrifying now, imagine what he must have been at full weight!" During the Second World War, when he was Eisenhower's Chief of Staff, Smith had weighed about 185, but an operation for stomach ulcers had reduced his size by about fifty pounds.

With the Eisenhower administration in 1953, followed by the armistice in Korea, the intelligence community moved into a new phase. The new Director of Central Intelligence, Allen W. Dulles, was the brother of the Secretary of State, and together they had the backing of the President. This did not automatically eliminate problems of coordination with the military services, but it helped. It was a period of consolidation after the rapid expansion during the Korean War, of emphasis on the development of professionalism in the intelligence services, of an increasing impact of the technological revolution, and of innovation. It was the period of the U-2 aircraft, which provided new information on Russian capabilities—information that had a major impact on estimates of Soviet strength. It was also a phase in which political action, or covert operation as typified by the Bay of Pigs, which originated during this administration, was looked on as a possible method for attaining national objectives. The Intelligence Advisory Committee became the United States Intelligence Board with an expanded substructure of committees to assist in the process of centralization and coordination. An intensive study of the foreign intelligence activities of the United States was ordered by President Eisenhower, although it remained for the Kennedy administration to implement the recommendations made as a result of this review.

From the viewpoint of some, perhaps the most important contribution of the Eisenhower/Dulles era was the establishment of mechanisms to review the work of the intelligence community, most of which remain in one form or another to this day. Impetus for establishing some process of review was provided by the report of the second Hoover Commission in 1955 and the concern of some Senators over the scope of intelligence activities, which seemed to have gone beyond the original intent of the Congress in creating the CIA. It was concern that Congress might establish a Joint Committee on CIA that led President Eisenhower to take action. In 1956 a President's Board of Consultants on Foreign Intelligence Activities was established to maintain a continual review of the entire intelligence structure on behalf of the Chief Executive. The Congress was well along in establishing permanent subcommittees to review the work of the community: in both the Senate and the House the chairmen of the Appropriations and Armed Services committees designated specific members to assist them in maintaining a regular review of CIA activities. The Bureau of the Budget broadened its examination of intelligence expenditures.

Allen Dulles, who succeeded General Smith as DCI, had a totally different personality than his predecessor. A former law partner of his brother, who had served a stint in the Foreign Service, he had been the most successful American intelligence operative in the Second World War. When based in Bern, Switzerland, he had been able to recruit agents from the top levels of the German government. Allen Dulles was a man of great charm and outgoing personality who much preferred to be the "case officer" for important operations or to engage in personal dealings with his own people or the heads of foreign intelligence services to the much less enjoyable tasks of coordinating the U.S. intelligence community or even the competing interests within the CIA. One of his favorite lieutenants described the operational side of the CIA under Dulles as "a group of warring baronies."

The shock of the disaster at the Bay of Pigs in April 1961 led to a new chapter in the history of the intelligence community. Following the failure of that operation, President John F. Kennedy asked General Maxwell Taylor to chair a high-level body composed of Attorney General Robert Kennedy, former Chief of Naval Operations Admiral Arleigh Burke, and DCI Allen Dulles to ascertain the reasons for the failure. The President reactivated, under a new name, the Foreign Intelligence Advisory Board, established by his predecessor, and asked it to examine the intelligence system carefully. Shortly thereafter he named John Alex McCone as the new Director of Central Intelligence.

It was during this period that a major change was made in the military intelligence segment of the intelligence community. A Defense Intelligence Agency was created in August 1961 to assist in the coordination of military intelligence and to serve directly the needs of the Secretary of Defense, the Joint Chiefs of Staff, and the unified and specified commands. It was not envisioned as another staff layer on top of the existing echelons in the Pentagon, nor was it intended to replace the Army, Navy, or Air Force Intelligence services so essential to those arms. The DIA was conceived as an organization to assist in the coordination of the military contributions to national estimates, to produce the current intelligence essential to the top officials of the Defense establishment, and to supervise the military intelligence collection effort in order to eliminate duplication. The three service intelligence agencies (Army, Navy, and Air Force) were to continue to process the specialized intelligence essential to their services.

Like any reorganization, the creation of DIA solved some problems and created others. The services felt they had suffered seriously in losing the estimative function, but the civilian agencies, mainly the CIA and State, were not unhappy to have most of the differences between the military services resolved in the Pentagon rather than in USIB subcommittees. It seemed reasonable to believe that if the Army or Navy or Air Force felt strongly enough about a difference with DIA, the issue would surface at the USIB. Other problems were on such jurisdictional issues as to which agency should compile intelligence on such matters as order of battle (the location and composition of other nations' armies, navies, and air forces), installations, transportation, etc.—the Defense Intelligence Agency or the individual military services.

Three years after the organization of the Defense Intelligence Agency, the USIB was streamlined, with the DIA representing the Pentagon, although the military services remained as observers with a right to footnote National Intelligence Estimates. The USIB will be discussed in greater detail later.

John McCone brought to the intelligence community vast experience in both government and industry. One of his first moves was to launch a study of his job as Director of Central Intelligence and as Director of the CIA and of the intelligence community. He sought and received President Kennedy's reaffirmation of his authority to coordinate the nation's intelligence activities, issued in the form of an unclassified letter for all to see.[17] He

[17] See Appendix.

created a deputy directorate in the CIA for science and technology and strengthened the command review structure of the agency. He provided strong and decisive leadership to the USIB. He enjoyed support in Congress and made it a practice to keep the appropriate congressional committees fully and frankly informed about all intelligence activities. He instituted and obtained passage of legislation effecting retirement benefits for certain CIA employees.

The fifth period of history of the intelligence community can be dated from 1965 to present. It could be called the Vietnam era because that war became the major preoccupation. If operational intelligence in Vietnam was often inadequate, the national estimates were good—if the published Pentagon Papers are an indication.

One obvious lesson of the Vietnam era is that the rest of the world does not stop while a war goes on. The intelligence community was expected to anticipate and report accurately and in detail on such developments as the turbulence and war in the Middle East, the Russian invasion of Czechoslovakia and the continual flux in Soviet relations in Eastern Europe, the cultural revolution in China, a revolt in Indonesia, and a number of other coups, attempted and successful.

John McCone was succeeded in 1965 by Vice Admiral William Raborn (USN Ret.), who fourteen months later was succeeded by Richard Helms, the first intelligence career officer to lead the intelligence community. In January 1973 Helms was succeeded by James Schlesinger, who had served as Chairman of the Atomic Energy Commission for a brief period.

This historical background is essential to an evaluation of the U.S. intelligence community. It is big—far bigger than William J. Donovan or the authors of the National Security Act of 1947 could have envisioned. The bigness

comes not from determined duplication or empire building (although there is some of that in any bureaucracy)
but from an information explosion, from the demand for
information that is difficult if not impossible to obtain,
and from the technological revolution which absorbs vast
quantities of manpower. Overseeing and exerting constant pressure to keep expenditures down (of both
manpower and money) are such bodies as the USIB, the
Office of Management and Budget, the congressional
committees, and the President's Foreign Intelligence
Advisory Board.

The agencies that constitute the intelligence commu-
nity are all part of the USIB structure. Chairing the USIB
is the Director of Central Intelligence in his capacity as
the President's representative and *not* as the head of CIA.
The Deputy Director of Central Intelligence sits on the
USIB as the CIA representative. Other members of the
USIB are the Director of the Defense Intelligence
Agency, the Director of the National Security Agency,
and, representing the State Department, the Director of
Intelligence and Research. President Nixon augmented
the USIB in 1971 by adding the Treasury Department, an
organization deeply concerned with international economy and monetary affairs. Acting as members of the
USIB when their interests are concerned are representatives of the Atomic Energy Commission and the FBI. The
chiefs of the military intelligence services regularly participate in USIB meetings.

The USIB is both a managerial and a substantive body.
As a substantive body, it gives the final review of
intelligence estimates that go to the President, insuring
that the projection presented is a community opinion and
not that of one agency. As a managerial body, the board,
with its numerous committees on which all intelligence
agencies can be represented, acts as the principal coordi-

nating mechanism for the community. The committee structure of the USIB that has evolved over the years now encompasses every aspect of the nation's foreign intelligence requirements, ranging from the methods of collection to all areas of research.

One such committee is that on overhead reconnaissance, which recommends those areas of the world where vital intelligence targets exist that need to be photographed; the final approval for such overflights must come from the policy level of the government. The USIB structure provides the community with probably the broadest and most comprehensive coordinating mechanism in the history of any nation's intelligence activities. Each agency shares its capabilities with the others, makes its claims for jurisdiction, accepts assignments on behalf of all, and exposes the results for community scrutiny. In a centralized and coordinated system, in which all information is available to all agencies regardless of who collected it or the degree of classification—on a need-to-know and compartmented security basis—the USIB knowledge of what it has to work with is indeed great.

In addition to the USIB committee structure as a means for coordinated control of the intelligence system, the Director of Central Intelligence has three other mechanisms to assist him in this complex task. The degree of complexity can be illustrated by a glance at the location in the government structure of the other intelligence agencies with which he must deal. The Defense Intelligence Agency reports to the Joint Chiefs of Staff and to the Secretary of Defense; the National Security Agency to an Assistant Secretary of Defense; the military intelligence agencies to the respective Chief of Staff of their service; thus in the Defense Department intelligence is at three different levels. The State Department intelligence representative is on the level of an Assistant

DEFENSE INTELLIGENCE AGENCY

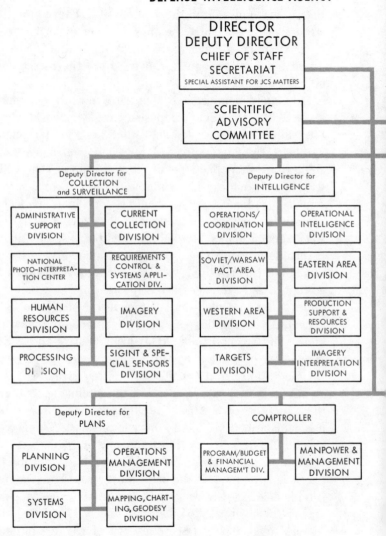

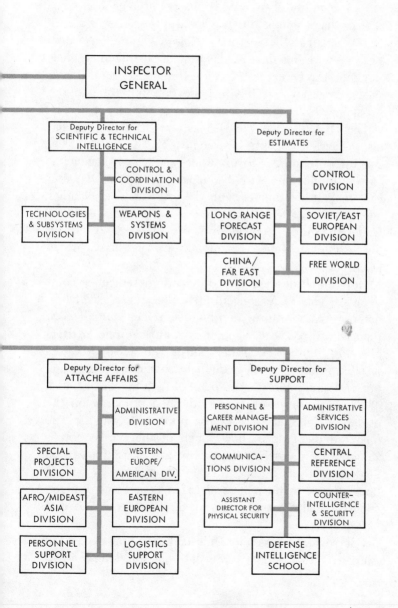

Secretary. The Justice Department representative is an
assistant to a Bureau Director. The Atomic Energy Commission member of the USIB reports to the general man-
ager of that commission. The Treasury member is a Special Assistant to the Secretary (National Security Affairs).
To cope with this intricate layering of command and liaison lines, the Director of Central Intelligence has his own
special high-level staff which devotes full time to the
problems of coordination.

The DCI also has the CIA as a coordinating mechanism. There is a liaison between each CIA office and the
equivalent component in other intelligence agencies:
current intelligence with its opposite number in DIA, and
INR in State; estimates with the estimators in all other
agencies; area divisions with State geographical desks.
Under the guidance of its directors, the DIA, in its now
ten years of existence, has organized along lines parallel
to CIA.

How much duplication exists in the intelligence community? The DIA concentrates almost exclusively on
defense-related information but also reviews intelligence
reports on political, economic, and scientific matters
affecting military considerations. The CIA produces
finished intelligence in many fields: scientific, economic,
political, and military. As a point of fact, the CIA's Office
of Strategic Research was established primarily on the
urging of Secretary of Defense Robert McNamara. The
final judgment as to how much of the duplication is
valuable for crosschecking and what is wasteful can be
made only by frequent dispassionate reviews by outside
bodies, such as the Office of Management and Budget,
congressional subcommittees, or the President's Board of
Consultants.

For several years the DCI had been urged by the
Bureau of the Budget (now the Office of Management

and Budget) to exert greater control over the expenditures of the other intelligence agencies in addition to his statutory responsibility for those of the CIA. On November 5, 1971, the White House announced that the DCI would head an Intelligence Resources Advisory Committee on which would be represented State, Defense, Budget, and CIA, and which would review the entire budget of the intelligence community. "Review" is not "control," but the DCI role is enhanced.

In summation, how has the concept of a coordinated system developed after nearly twenty-five years? It has evolved during a highly dynamic period of world history and in most instances has met the test, the test being how well has it served the policy-makers. There are some duplications; for example, military production of political intelligence in an age when commanders must have the knowledge of a diplomat as well as that of a soldier or sailor. But as anyone knows who has participated in bureaucratic battles, duplication is not eliminated by legislation but by persuasion and conviction: persuasion that the money can best be saved or spent elsewhere, and conviction that the other agencies can produce better intelligence on the same subject and be responsive to requests for its use, for example, the State Department producing and supplying political intelligence for the Defense Department.

What are the alternatives to the present system? One frequently suggested change is to put a "tsar" over the entire community with life-and-death powers of command. This approach has two major defects. In the first place, it would require the creation of a sizable new bureaucracy duplicating the existing agencies. Second, the "tsar" would have to possess supercabinet status. To exercise true command authority, he would have to outrank three department heads.

The other alternative often advanced is to combine all of the intelligence agencies under one roof. This idea would not work. Each of the departments needs an intelligence service to handle specialized requirements. The diversity adds strength to the system and provides a crosscheck that in itself is a valuable asset for national security. Even the combining of the CIA and DIA, as was once studied, would not result in a gain. The DIA, responsible to the Joint Chiefs of Staff and the Secretary of Defense, is primarily defense-oriented and mostly military. The CIA is the agency of the President producing national intelligence and is primarily civilian.

How good is the U.S. intelligence community? Obviously, it is neither omniscient nor ubiquitous, nor could it be. There are gaps in knowledge on vital subjects. But based on what was missing in 1947, compared to what is missing today, the record is good.

A critical viewpoint may be provided by an examination of the most important issues in the intelligence community and its role in our government and society. First, what controls have been established over the intelligence community? Are they effective? Perhaps as important, what is the impact of intelligence on policy? What are the overseas operations of the intelligence community, and how extensive are its activities within the United States? Where does the intelligence community find support in the United States? What are the areas of criticism? Finally, what is the proper role of intelligence in a free society? These questions are discussed in succeeding chapters.

2

The Government Structure: Accountability and Control

The President of the United States as the Commander-in-Chief of the Armed Forces and as the chief executive officer is in fact as well as in theory the principal recipient of the product of the intelligence community. Prior to the establishment of the central intelligence structure one could go further and say that the President was the chief intelligence officer of the government.

President Franklin Roosevelt, in the fall of 1941, received separate reports from at least four government departments on the deteriorating relations with Japan: Secretary of State Cordell Hull, who was directing intense diplomatic negotiations with Japanese ambassadors Nomura and Kurusu; intercepted cable traffic from the War and Navy departments on Japanese preparations for war; and memoranda from the FBI on the activities of Japanese agents in Hawaii and the United States. It was up to President Roosevelt to sift through all of this information and make his own estimate of the situation.

James MacGregor Burns describes Roosevelt's estimating process as follows: "Pinioned but not paralyzed. The President's mind was taken up by probabilities, calculations, guesses, alternatives . . . he felt that a Japanese attack south was probable . . . least probable—to the extent that he thought about it at all—in Hawaii." [1]

Under the modern system, it would be rare indeed if any "raw intelligence"—information not evaluated, analyzed, and assessed—reached the President. What the President receives from the intelligence community is a fine distillation of a great volume of information, a concise summary of the most important developments affecting the vital interests of the United States.

The selection of the material to go forward to the President is not haphazard or dependent on the interests or whims of subordinate officials. The Director of Central Intelligence is constantly in communication with the White House, on occasion with the President personally, most frequently with the Special Assistant for National Security Affairs. The DCI regularly attends meetings of the National Security Council and meets frequently with the Secretaries of State and Defense, the Chairman of the Joint Chiefs of Staff, and the Attorney General. The DCI thus can and does reflect to the CIA and the other intelligence agencies the concern and interests of the highest level of the government.

The President receives his intelligence information in a variety of ways. Under the general direction of the CIA, with the participation of State and Defense, a daily Central Intelligence Bulletin is prepared for the President and forwarded to him through the Special Assistant for National Security Affairs. The President may elect to read the bulletin in whole, in part, or have it presented orally by his assistant at a regular morning meeting. The Special Assistant will play a very key role in this process as he will also be the recipient of the daily DIA Intelligence Summary and material from the State Department, and his decision as to what the President

<hr>

[1] *Roosevelt—The Soldier of Freedom* (New York: Harcourt Brace Jovanovich, 1970), p. 159.

should see or hear, as well as his own interpretation, can have a major impact on the views of the chief executive. Needless to say, a lot will depend on the consistent credibility—or lack thereof—of the CIA and other intelligence agencies and the quality of the reports produced.

The daily bulletins are only part of the intelligence received by the President. Frequently, special reports or memoranda are requested or are produced on the initiative of the intelligence agencies. On occasion, one of the many hundreds of regular publications of the intelligence community, generally produced for the "working level" of the government, may have new information of such note that it should be seen at the highest level. Most important of all intelligence reports received at the White House are the National Intelligence Estimates.

The role of the Special Assistant for National Security Affairs has been mentioned above in connection with the handling of intelligence reports destined for the President. This position in the White House, created during the Eisenhower administration, has assumed increasing importance in the formulation of defense and foreign policy. The staff of the Special Assistant, now numbering more than a hundred senior officers assigned by State, Defense, CIA, and other departments and agencies and recruited from private life, has become the most senior body in the government using the information and intelligence received to formulate policy proposals for the consideration of the National Security Council and the President.

The President's concern with intelligence goes beyond his requirement for essential information. He is responsible for the effectiveness of the controls over the CIA and the intelligence community. As specified in the National Security Act of 1947, the CIA reports to the National

Security Council. The President is Chairman of the NSC and the staff of that advisory body is in the office of his Special Assistant for National Security Affairs. In view of this and the secret and sensitive nature of intelligence, the requirement for the President to play a direct and personal role in the review of the management and competence of the CIA and the intelligence community is more demanding than that for the other departments and agencies of the Executive Branch.

President John F. Kennedy, at the swearing-in ceremony for John McCone in November 1961, commented on the vital role played by intelligence in formulating policy that seemed to be always under attack. He held out his hand to the new Director of Central Intelligence and said, "Welcome to the bull's-eye!" A few months later McCone took to the White House the man he had selected to be his deputy, Major General Marshall S. Carter; Carter was to have been named to command of one of the continental armies. The President told Carter: "General, commanding an army is an important job. Running the Defense Department is even more important and difficult. But running the CIA is just about as difficult and tough a job as there is."

In his immediate office the President has several means for review and evaluation of the intelligence community. The one with the sharpest cutting edge is the Office of Management and Budget. This is the President's machinery for controlling the expenditures of the executive branch of the government. He personally gives this office instructions as to the size of the budget, which is then allocated among the departments and agencies; he may even specify amounts for particular agencies or activities. Units of the office examine in detail the budget proposals of all of the intelligence agencies, including the most sensitive operations of the Central Intelligence Agency.

In 1968 a National Intelligence Review Board was established under the chairmanship of the Deputy Director of Central Intelligence, with State and DIA as members. Its mission was to review all major intelligence collection and processing efforts for relevancy, effectiveness, and expense. Although the establishment of this review board was personally and officially approved by the Secretaries of State and Defense, its efforts were vitiated to some degree by the opposition of members of the intelligence community whose operations would have been curtailed. NSA, especially, was effective in securing support from the Deputy Secretary of Defense in combating cutbacks, the Deputy Director of Defense for Research and Engineering helped fight recommendations for curtailment of expenditures for overhead reconnaissance.

The November 1971 Presidential order reemphasized the authority of the Director of Central Intelligence to examine the budgets of all of the foreign intelligence units of the government, an order which carried a mandate to cut costs and improve the output.[2] The proposal was not a new one. Several directors of the budget had urged previous DCI's to take an active role in reviewing the expenditures of the other intelligence agencies.

In November 1971, while increasing the authority of the DCI, the President created a new subcommittee of the National Security Council to determine how well the intelligence produced was meeting the requirements of the policy-makers of the government. The Special Assistant for National Security Affairs was designated chairman of this subcommittee, and its members included the

[2] See Benjamin Welles, "Helms Told to Cut Global Expenses," *The New York Times*, November 7, 1971.

Director of Central Intelligence, the Under Secretary of State, Deputy Secretary of Defense, Chairman of the Joint Chiefs of Staff, and the Attorney General. The composition of this body was similar to the committee known under a variety of names that for many years had reviewed for the President all covert operations, proposed or in being, and in later years all major collection actions. In effect, the 1971 order established under the National Security Council a single review mechanism over all activities of the intelligence community ranging from collection to covert operations.[3]

Government committees are not noted as the most effective decision-making bodies. All too often they become treaty-making bodies negotiating agreements between co-equal participants, each battling to protect his own organization, yielding as little as possible, and accepting the lowest common denominator. On the other hand, government committees can be effective if chaired by an official who has the full backing of the President, plus the personal courage to force through measures that curtail jurisdictions or require economies which are certain to be unpopular with all affected.

The President has a third major group to review on his behalf the effectiveness of the CIA and the intelligence community: the Foreign Intelligence Advisory Board. Established in 1956 by President Eisenhower at a time when there was considerable pressure in Congress, led by Senator Mike Mansfield of Montana, for a joint committee on intelligence, this board has been continued by each new administration. Its charter requires it to review the work of the CIA and other intelligence agencies on a regular basis and to report to the President not less than twice a year. Its members are chosen by the President

---

[3] For further discussion of covert operations, see Chapter 4.

from private life and have included distinguished businessmen, scientists, and retired diplomats, admirals, and generals. Among the many who have served on this board are James Killian, former president of the Massachusetts Institute of Technology and the board's first chairman; Clark Clifford, close adviser to Presidents Truman, Kennedy, and Johnson and a former Secretary of Defense; Colgate Darden, former Governor of Virginia, Chancellor of the University of Virginia, and six times Congressman; career diplomat and former Under Secretary of State Robert Murphy; Joseph P. Kennedy; Admiral Richard Connolly; and Generals Maxwell Taylor and James Doolittle, and many others of similar caliber. The board has a small full-time staff located in the executive offices of the President.

It has been argued that the President's Foreign Intelligence Advisory Board does not supply a sufficiently critical review; that its members are all from the "establishment" and therefore likely to endorse most, if not all, activities that the CIA and other agencies engage in; and that it does not have the background or expertise to make meaningful evaluations. These allegations are difficult to refute in a public discussion, as the board's findings and recommendations are seldom published. However, it is my view that such criticisms are invalid and are based more on prejudice than knowledge.[4]

The argument that the board is simply a mirror of the system ignores the broad experience of the members. It is a grave error to assume that because an individual served in the government he is an advocate of all that the intelligence agencies may do. Most board members are more familiar with the weaknesses than the strengths of

---

[4] One of my responsibilities between 1956 and 1962 was that of liaison officer between the CIA and the President's Foreign Intelligence Advisory Board.

the intelligence system. This background gives them the required expertise, that of intelligence consumers. It is quite true that none of the board members represents the views of the Communist party or the radicals of the right or the left. Finally, it was my experience that the President's board was one of the severest critics of the intelligence system. It is noteworthy that many of its recommendations were adopted or served as the basis for later reorganizations.

Before leaving the subject of the White House, a word should be said about the Secret Service, the organization charged with the protection of the President. The U.S. Secret Service is in the Treasury Department. In its responsibility to insure the safety of the President and his family, the Secret Service is supported by all other departments and agencies of the government, but most especially by the FBI, the CIA, and the military intelligence agencies. These agencies pool all information on potential threats to the President from subversives, dissidents, cranks, or the emotionally disturbed. When the President travels abroad, the Secret Service sends an advance party and depends very heavily on the CIA and the security service of the host government.

The use of such information by the Secret Service is but one small area where the intelligence community's product plays an important role in the government. In the Treasury Department alone, foreign intelligence information is used in economic analysis. In turn, Treasury supplies to the intelligence agencies such basic information as it acquires through its channels. With an adverse balance of payments and the state of the dollar a major concern in U.S. foreign relations, the necessity for complete and comprehensive economic intelligence has assumed even greater importance; thus the new role of the Treasury Department as a member of the intelligence community and the emphasis on economic intelligence.

The State Department is a large consumer of intelligence in the government and also one of the principal control mechanisms over the intelligence community. This department has a limited intelligence organization of its own under the Director of Intelligence and Research. He provides the secretary's morning staff meeting with the latest important material from intelligence channels, acts as the principal department liaison to the intelligence agencies, sits as a member of the USIB, and directs analysis of intelligence reports and the preparation of background papers for the policy desks. Over the years, the sizable Research and Analysis Branch, transferred from the OSS to State in 1945, has dwindled as more and more functions were transferred back to the CIA or to the area bureaus in the department.

Intelligence reports from the CIA flow into the State Department at every echelon and on all subjects of interest to the department. The regional bureaus receive pertinent raw intelligence reports, area analyses, and national estimates. These are in addition to the regular reporting from the ambassadors and the Foreign and Consular Services. CIA area office chiefs attend the regular weekly staff meetings of the assistant secretaries, both to insure careful coordination on all matters of mutual interest and to discuss substantive matters. Thus, the State Department has three echelons on which to exercise its influence and control: through the Secretary as a member of the National Security Council, through the Under Secretary, who represents the department on the NSC subcommittees on intelligence and operations, and in the direct liaison at the Assistant Secretary level. In Chapter 4 there will be an analysis of the controls exerted by ambassadors in U.S. missions abroad.

The Defense Department is not only the major con-

sumer of the intelligence dollar—87.5 percent of the total
amount spent on intelligence in 1969—but as the largest
department in the government it presents the most
complex problem of control and accountability. Former
Secretary Robert McNamara is reported to have said
once that he discovered intelligence items in at least
nineteen different budgets within the department. To
describe the overall problem in Defense as one of the
most difficult management problems in the world would
not be an overstatement.

Within Defense, communications intelligence, including NSA and the agencies in the three military services,
takes a very large proportion of the overall costs for
intelligence. Photographic satellites are expensive. Personnel at all levels of the military services from the
intelligence staffs in Washington to the battalion S-2's in
the field add to the cost. There has even been discussion
as to whether reconnaissance aircraft or scouting subma-
rines should not be in the intelligence budget.

The Secretary of Defense looks to the Defense Intelligence Agency for information of special interest on
military matters and to the USIB for estimates of
developments in areas of vital national interest. He looks
to the Director of Central Intelligence to coordinate the
national intelligence effort, including those matters relat-
ing to defense. Within the Defense Department controls
are exercised at a number of levels.

The senior civilian intelligence official in the Defense
Department is an Assistant Secretary of Defense for
Intelligence, a post created in November 1971. This
officer is responsible for coordination of policy and for
cost monitoring, especially in the collection of intelligence. Former Deputy Secretary David Packard in
announcing the appointment said that this would entail
examining "the adequacy of strategic intelligence gather-

ing about enemy weapons and the question of whether too much money is spent gathering that data." [5] It was clear from the announcement of the creation of the position that it would have limited authority over the five major intelligence components of the Defense Department. Intelligence coordination in the department previously had been located in such offices as the Assistant Secretary for Administration (a post no longer in existence), the Deputy Assistant Secretary for International Security Affairs, and that of a Special Assistant to the Secretary. The Assistant Secretary of Defense (Comptroller) also can play an important role in the coordination of intelligence if so authorized by the secretary.

The Defense Intelligence Agency, reporting to the secretary and the Joint Chiefs of Staff, coordinates the defense contribution to national intelligence estimates and the production of current intelligence (the day-to-day reporting on international events of importance) and produces intelligence on many military subjects. The DIA also manages the Defense attaché program for the training and assignment of military attachés to the U.S. embassies, although the individual services nominate the personnel for the program. The DIA also has the herculean assignment of coordinating the issuance of requests for intelligence collection (known as "requirements" in intelligence jargon)—herculean in that intelligence organizations are insatiable in their demands for all information about every subject under the sun. Here the authority of the DIA ends. The Director of DIA must persuade the Joint Chiefs of Staff to support him in any jurisdictional issue involving the individual services, a difficult task when each of the Joint Chiefs has his own

---

[5] "New Post Filled in Intelligence," *The New York Times*, November 5, 1971.

intelligence service reporting directly to him—except for the Chairman of the Joint Chiefs, who stands above such matters but who obviously cannot shed decades of loyalty to his own service. The DIA has a dual constituency: the secretary and his civilian assistants and the Joint Chiefs of Staff and the unified commands such as CINCEUR, Commander-in-Chief, Europe, commanding all Army, Navy, and Air Force units.

Of the other intelligence components in Defense, the National Security Agency reports to the Secretary of Defense. The Army, Navy, and Air Force intelligence units are directly under their respective Chiefs of Staff. Outside of Washington, each military command has its own intelligence unit directly under the control of that unit commander. To illustrate the complexity of the problem, in Europe the Commander-in-Chief (CINC) of the U.S. Army, Europe, has his own intelligence staff, as does the CINC of the U.S. Air Force, Europe. These headquarters report to CINCEUR, who also has an intelligence staff and who reports directly to the Joint Chiefs of Staff. At the risk of confusing but to be quite correct and further illustrate the complexity, the CINC, U.S. Army, Europe, also reports to the Chief of Staff of the U.S. Army in Washington, to whom he looks for personnel, equipment, etc., although he is under the field command of CINCEUR.

A civilian might well look at this command structure and make the quick judgment that the only way to eliminate such duplication and expense is to do away with all intelligence staffs except those in Washington. Those in Europe would be quick to say that this would be exactly backwards and that it should be the Washington units that are eliminated. These cuts might well be the most efficient solution in a business organization, but it would not work in military units where the mission is to fight battles and win wars.

A quick look at the practical and human considerations may explain why some aspects of the present organizational system for intelligence are unavoidable. Take the situation of the Seventh U.S. Army in Germany as a prototype of a military unit in the field. The commanding general of that army is responsible for the defense of a specific geographical area. He looks to his intelligence staff to keep him advised of all threats to that area from any direction and to give him enough information about any potential enemy so that he can ask for sufficient forces and equipment to defend the command. It is safe to say that any commander would insist that he must have intelligence resources under his command just as he has infantrymen, artillery, ammunition, trucks, and medical supplies. While his intelligence staff may depend on the CIA, on other commands, or on friendly services for some information, it is that staff's responsibility to see that the intelligence is available. The same principles can be used in explaining the intelligence staffs at each echelon up the ladder.

The question may then be asked: Is there no way to reduce the duplication and expense of a large military intelligence effort? The answer is "yes," but the effort must be rationally and practically applied.

The intelligence staffs in the military services accurately reflect the affluence or poverty of the current budget. Intelligence has never been the favorite son in the military; more often the runt of the litter. Duplication and expenses within or between the services can be eliminated by careful surgery. The collection effort, for example, must have central control over all sources, particularly the most expensive ones: photo-reconnaissance and communications intelligence. (There is a most difficult line to be drawn between what is duplicated and superfluous and what is necessary for security. Because it is difficult is no reason it should not be done.) But when one speaks of limiting collection, the crunch issue is who will tell the commands in the field what collection to eliminate. The scenario is not hard to see: Washington says there is no need to fly photographic coverage over quadrant X-2; the field intelligence chief tells his commanding general that he worries about what the "hoodwinks" are doing in quadrant X-2. Who prevails? It is enough to keep the commanding general, his intelligence chief, and a few in Washington awake at night. "Do we want security or economy?" will be the cry from the field, and Washington's reassuring words that the hoodwinks are quiet at the moment will not still the controversy.

A second major area where economies can be effected in the intelligence system is in the processing of the information once it is collected. If an item of intelligence is collected in Germany, it seems obvious to say that the first unit that wants to see it, analyze it, and use it for decision-making is the unit in Germany. But the same item will go through much the same process at CINCEUR and in many places in Washington.

Military intelligence is not concerned solely with potential foreign adversaries. The services are responsible both for the physical protection of their installations in the continental limits of the United States and for the security and loyalty of all personnel. Further, the Army may be called on to restore civil order, as when elements of the 82nd Airborne Division were sent to Washington during the riots of 1967. This responsibility led the Army "by direction of competent civilian authority" to develop a massive and controversial file of individuals considered to be potential troublemakers.

The statutory authority for the use of the Army to "insure domestic tranquillity," as it is phrased in the preamble to the Constitution, is based on Article II, Section 1, "The executive power shall be vested in a President . . ."; Section 2, "The President shall be Commander in Chief of the Army and Navy . . ."; and Article IV, Section 4, "The United States shall . . . protect each of them [the states] . . . against domestic violence." The role of the Congress in such actions is insured by Article I, Section 8 of the Constitution, which requires that body "to make rules for the government and regulation of the land and naval forces."

The organization primarily charged with information on the internal security of the United States is the Federal Bureau of Investigation of the Justice Department, whose activities come constantly under the scrutiny of the courts and are directly under the Attorney General.

Of all the controls and review mechanisms over the intelligence community, potentially the most powerful is the Congress of the United States. The modern history, however, of congressional overview of the intelligence system is fraught with controversy. Has there been adequate surveillance? Is any review really possible? Within Congress, a jurisdictional issue in the Senate as to whether the Armed Services Committee should share its responsibilities as the parent committee of the CIA and the military intelligence staffs with the Foreign Relations Committee put the CIA and the issue of review and control in the crossfire between contending chairmen in Congress.

Under the law, Congress has unquestioned authority to review even the most highly sensitive work of all of the intelligence agencies. The bureaucratic adage of "What Congress gives it can take away" applies to this area of

government as well as to the rest of the executive branch.
The issue is not so much one of authority as it is the
reluctance of the members of Congress to get into
sensitive intelligence matters, the lack of time available
to do the job, and the relative priority for such an effort,
compared with many other issues of both greater immedi-
acy and more political impact. It takes a U-2 incident or a
Bay of Pigs to make intelligence the main issue before the
Congress, although over the years there has always been
a handful of members who have advocated greater
scrutiny of the secret agencies.

On several occasions, the Congress has addressed the
question of whether it was properly organized to review
the work of the CIA and the intelligence community. For
several years Senator Mike Mansfield was the principal
proponent of the establishment of a joint committee on
intelligence. Among the original co-sponsors were such
distinguished Senators as John F. Kennedy and Lyndon
B. Johnson, who, later, as incumbents of the White
House, were firmly to oppose any such committee.
During the early fifties there were also similar bills
introduced by various members of the House of Representatives, which, as a body, generally does not favor
joint committees.

Senator Mansfield first introduced a bill for a joint
committee on intelligence in the 82nd Congress, and
when it failed to pass, he reintroduced it in the 83rd
Congress in 1955, noting that there had been "almost no
Congressional inspection" of the CIA since it had been
established in 1947. This point was not accepted by
Senator Richard Russell of Georgia, Chairman of the
Armed Services Committee, who reported that senior
members of his group had looked into the CIA from time
to time. Mansfield acknowledged the need for secrecy in
the matter.

This initial skirmish was to characterize much of the congressional debate that continued sporadically for the next twelve years: the advocates of a joint committee insisting that their objective was not to unveil the secrecy of intelligence operations but to insure deeper and more formal review by a body representing a more diversified membership of the Congress; their opponents stressing that such a review was already taking place and that the effort was one that infringed on their jurisdiction.

In 1955, at the time Senator Mansfield reintroduced his bill, two reviews of CIA activities were in progress. A task force of the second Hoover Commission, under the chairmanship of General Mark Wayne Clark, was examining the intelligence community. The Hoover Commission included members of Congress as well as the public. Another study group under the chairmanship of General James Doolittle, independent of the Clark Task Force and appointed by the President, looked at the secret operations of the CIA. The Clark Task Force issued two reports, one public and one classified, while the Doolittle Group report was top secret and its contents have never been disclosed.

As previously mentioned, in January 1956 President Eisenhower established the Board of Consultants on Foreign Intelligence Activities (later to be called the Foreign Intelligence Advisory Board) under the chairmanship of James Killian, an action interpreted by some as one calculated to assist the opponents of a joint congressional committee.

The Mansfield Bill reached the floor of the Senate for debate on April 9, 1956. Senate passage seemed to be likely as there were thirty-five co-sponsors. However, a formidable opposition coalesced around Senator Russell, including former National Security Council members Alben W. Barkley (when he was Vice President) and

Stuart Symington (when he was Secretary of the Air Force);[6] fourteen of the co-sponsors deserted Senator Mansfield and the bill was defeated by a vote of 59 to 27.

While the major issue involved was congressional review of the activities of the executive branch, most specifically of the conduct of foreign relations, the two-day debate was enlivened by the allegations of Senator Joseph McCarthy of Wisconsin of Communist infiltration and other malfeasance in the CIA and became in most respects a power struggle between the standing committees and those critical of the work of those bodies.

Although bills calling for an intelligence committee were introduced in both houses in each session of Congress, there was no major debate again until 1960. When a U-2 aircraft on a photo-reconnaissance mission over the Soviet Union was shot down on May 1, 1960, the Soviet Union used the occasion for a propaganda campaign against the United States and walked out of a summit meeting. The U.S. government did not assist matters by attempting a cover story that the plane was on a weather-sampling mission of the National Aviation and Space Administration, a fiction which was quickly disproven when the Russians produced the plane, the pilot, and the cameras. President Eisenhower then acknowledged that it was a photographic mission flown with his approval.

The Senate Foreign Relations Committee held an inquiry into the U-2 operations. As a result, Senator Mansfield proposed on the floor of the Senate on June 23, 1960, a major reorganization of the policy-making machinery of the executive branch. He suggested the abolition of the National Security Council and the

[6] The original NSC included the military service secretaries as members. When the Secretary of Defense became a member in 1949, the service secretaries were dropped.

creation of an Inner Cabinet Council in its place, the placing of the foreign aid and information agencies under the State Department,[7] the creation of a State–Defense committee to advise the President on all intelligence matters, the transfer from the CIA of all nonclandestine intelligence collection, and the establishment of a joint committee of Congress on the CIA.

In 1960 the House of Representatives was the locale of another brief skirmish in the jurisdictional issue of review of intelligence activities. In August it became public knowledge that two employees of the National Security Agency had disappeared and were believed to have gone to a Communist country. William H. Martin and Bernon F. Mitchell had taken leave on June 24. When they had not returned nor sent word of their whereabouts by July 18, NSA started an investigation, which revealed that Martin and Mitchell had defected to the Soviet Union.

When the news first reached Congress that two officers were missing from one of the government's most sensitive agencies, there was consternation, not lessened any by the lack of information about where the men had gone or how much they knew about NSA's accomplishments in intercepting and deciphering the communications of other nations. If they talked about their work publicly, at a minimum it could be embarrassing to the United States, and at the worst damaging to national security.

On September 1 Congressman Francis E. Walter introduced a resolution in the House authorizing the House Committee on Un-American Activities to conduct "a full and complete study" of each of the intelligence agencies. The House adjourned the same day without passing the resolution. On September 7 Chairman Carl

[7] The Agency for International Development and the United States Information Agency, while maintaining their autonomy, later were placed under the Secretary of State for policy guidance.

Vinson of the Armed Services Committee named a three-man subcommittee to conduct a "complete investigation" of the intelligence agencies "without publicity." Mr. Vinson made the issue clear in a statement to the press: "The Committee on Armed Services has jurisdiction over these matters, and the Committee will exercise its jurisdiction. This is the Committee charged by the Congress with the responsibility for looking into matters of this nature." [8] Congressman Walters did not pursue the issue.

In March 1961 resolutions were again introduced in the House for a joint committee on intelligence but were not reported out of the Rules Committee. On April 27, some ten days after the Bay of Pigs, Senator Eugene McCarthy of Minnesota introduced a similar bill in the Senate.

The issue of intelligence overview was taken up again in the House in 1963 and 1964 with several bills introduced for a joint committee. In 1963 Congressman George Mahon of the Appropriations Committee spoke against any more revelations of intelligence activities. In 1964 nineteen representatives introduced proposals for a joint congressional committee on intelligence; but two powers in the House, Clarence Cannon, the Chairman of the Appropriations Committee, and Leslie Arends of the Armed Services Committee, defended the system, especially against charges made in an article in *Esquire* magazine by the then Congressman from New York, John V. Lindsay.

In 1965 Representative James H. Scheuer of New York introduced a proposal to establish a congressional commission on the role of Congress in foreign policy and intelligence activities, and Senator Eugene McCarthy

[8] Washington *Post*, September 8, 1960, p. 1.

proposed a select Senate committee to conduct a year-long analysis of the CIA. Neither was adopted, but in January 1966 the Chairman of the Senate Foreign Relations Committee placed on the tentative agenda of that body a proposed study of the CIA's impact on foreign policy. By May the issue once again had become a major power struggle in Congress.

On May 17 the Foreign Relations Committee, by a vote of 14 to 5, approved a resolution which would create a nine-member Committee on Intelligence Operations, composed of three members from each of three committees: Armed Services, Appropriations, and Foreign Relations. The Chairman of the Armed Services Committee denounced the action: "There is no justification whatever for any other committee to muscle in on the jurisdiction of the Armed Services Committee so far as the CIA is concerned." The Senator went on to denounce an editorial in *The New York Times* which stated that the CIA acted independently of the State Department and that it also influenced the selection of the congressional members of its subcommittee.[9] The battle lines extended from the senior body over into the House, and the chairmen of that body's Armed Services and Appropriations Committees announced their opposition to the proposals in the Senate.

The Senate Majority Leader, Mike Mansfield, who had once been a proponent of a joint bill but now maintained a neutral position, tried to mediate to avoid a floor fight. "The debate wouldn't help the agency (CIA) or wouldn't help the Senate. I am fearful that things would be said that shouldn't be said." Together with the Minority Leader, Everett Dirksen, he discussed the fight with President Johnson.

[9] *The New York Times*, May 17, 1966, p. 1.

Mansfield also offered compromises. One would add senior members of the Foreign Relations Committee to the seven-member group chaired by Senator Richard Russell, a proposal which the latter did not then accept. A second suggestion was to establish a CIA subcommittee in Foreign Relations, a move which Chairman J. William Fulbright said would not work because the CIA Director, Vice Admiral William Raborn, had already said he would not provide the same information he gave to Armed Services to the Foreign Relations Committee.

On July 14, 1965, the Senate debated the issue for four and a half hours. After the first hour Senator Mansfield proposed a closed session—the first in three years—after which by a vote of 61 to 28, with party lines split, the proposal was referred to the Armed Services Committee, where it died. Six months later Senator Russell invited Senators Fulbright, Bourke Hickenlooper, and Mansfield of the Foreign Relations Committee to attend all watch-dog committee sessions regardless of the subject.

As a result of this arrangement, the congressional review of intelligence activities is concentrated in four subcommittees: one each from the Armed Services and Appropriations Committees in each House of Congress. Three members of the Foreign Relations Committee sit with the Armed Services subcommittee in the Senate. In addition, the Senate Foreign Relations Committee receives briefings by the CIA. There have been proposals that Congress be provided with the same intelligence estimates and analyses given the White House. In July 1971 Senator John Sherman Cooper introduced a bill that would require the CIA "fully and currently" to provide Congress with both intelligence information and evaluations affecting foreign relations and national security.

The degree and extent of the review by the congressional committees are not well documented, as reports are rarely published. In the congressional calendar, the committees occasionally indicate their meetings with the CIA and other intelligence agencies. Sometimes brief reports are given to the media on the general subjects covered. There have been a few reports published on congressional hearings on intelligence.[10] This congressional method of review leaves many dissatisfied: probably a number of the 515 members who are not on intelligence subcommittees and a certain proportion of the public.

Leaving aside jurisdictional issues between congressional committees, and the classic struggle between the legislative and executive branches over the conduct of foreign relations, what is the principal problem of congressional controls over the intelligence community? Basically, it is the necessity to restrict information in order to maintain secrecy.

Perhaps it is advisable to examine first why such secrecy is required in intelligence operations. The most sensitive aspect of intelligence work is the source of information. Such information in descending order of importance concerns the following major areas.

First, intentions: What are the long- and short-range objectives of a given country and how does it intend to achieve them? Will it resort to subversion and war or will it use diplomacy, trade, and other peaceful methods? Are such intentions representative of the national will or solely those of the party or group in power, and if the latter, what change in intentions will occur if another group or party comes to power? Are those in power likely to act rationally in times of stress or challenge, or are they inclined to be impetuous and take chances?

---

[10] The thirty-nine-volume Pearl Harbor Investigation (Washington: Government Printing Office, 1946) contains the most information on intelligence ever published by Congress.

It can be seen that information on a nation's intentions is not easy to obtain. It is not likely to be available in one document, although many types of papers could provide such information: minutes of cabinet meetings, foreign office position papers, instructions to defense departments, war plans, etc. Frequently such information is only in the minds of the men who make the decisions. Access to such information can come only from a human agent—one of the decision-makers, an assistant or clerk, or a close confidant of one in power, in short, a spy. If the spy's employers reveal the information, his career is likely to terminate abruptly. It is not too difficult to ascertain the leak when information is held on such a limited basis.

The second type of information which governments try to conceal as much as possible, and which therefore becomes a target for intelligence operations, is research and development. In an age in which technological breakthrough can have a decisive effect on national security, clues as to the nature and direction of a nation's research are of great value in assessing future capabilities. The espionage efforts of the Russians against the nuclear research programs of the United States and Great Britain are illustrative.

A third, and perhaps the most obvious, guarded information is that on new technology, which serves to increase the strength of a nation. New steel mills, petroleum refineries, and chemical complexes are difficult to conceal even in closed societies, but advanced weapons such as aircraft, ships, and tanks are a different matter. The advent of the photographic satellite has made concealment a more difficult but not impossible task. All missiles, satellites, and objects in space are observed. Aircraft and smaller weapons can be kept under cover while the camera is overhead, but shipyards and missile silos (the latter during construction) are difficult to hide.

This short summary may serve to illustrate that exposure not only of the method of collection but of the information itself can adversely affect intelligence. It is a constant struggle between security on the one hand and intelligence on the other. As knowledge of each new intelligence technique becomes available, the other side concentrates on methods to protect its information and frustrate that means of collection. As evidence of another nation's knowledge is revealed, every effort is made to prevent the escape of further information.

The following rather elementary equations may serve to make the point.

Method of Collection	*Protection Against*
Espionage (spies)	1. Confine access to secret information to smallest possible number of individuals.
	2. Insure, beyond question, security and loyalty of all persons with access to information.
	3. Keep documents under most secure conditions and record time, place, and name of each reader.
	4. If possible, keep documents and individuals under constant surveillance.
	5. Compartmentalize.
Photographic (aircraft and satellite)	1. Build a roof over everything you do and conceal heat emanations (to avoid infrared detection).
	2. Put sensitive items (planes, tanks, etc.) under cover when satellites or planes are about.
	3. If concealment is impossible, camouflage to confuse.
Communications (mail,	1. Don't communicate.

telephone, telegraph, radio, television)

2. If you must communicate, send by human messenger (but the message still may be intercepted without your knowledge).
3. If you cannot send by a messenger, use a system or code in which only the sender and receiver can understand the true message.

Thus, the extreme sensitivity to the spread of knowledge about intelligence activities expressed in the congressional debates was not a specious argument advanced to bolster a jurisdictional position. As Senator Russell and others have stated with accuracy, if intelligence operations are to be public it would be best to abolish the organizations because their work would soon be valueless.

The specific congressional review of the intelligence community looks primarily into three matters: money, area of activity, and results. The Appropriations subcommittee members go into considerable detail, according to the availability of their time, examining the budgets and actual expenditures of all of the agencies. Their concerns are whether the money is spent for activities that are authorized, whether the results are worthwhile, and whether the effort is unique or duplicative. On many occasions the committee will ask for additional and detailed justification before approving all or part of the appropriation. It is known that the committee has been highly critical of duplicative collection efforts in the military intelligence field.[11]

---

[11] As Inspector General of the CIA from 1953 to 1961, I was also given the responsibility for general supervision of the agency's liaison with the Congress. As the Executive Director from 1962 to 1965, I held the same responsibility and, in addition, assisted in the preparation and presentation of the agency's budget to the Appropriations committees.

The Armed Services subcommittees, while cognizant and occasionally critical of the budget and expenditures, are primarily concerned with the organization and actual operations of the intelligence community. The Director of Central Intelligence and the chiefs of the other intelligence agencies make it a practice to keep this committee informed of what operations are taking place (in general, and not with specific names of sources) and what problems are encountered.

The subcommittee members from the Senate Foreign Relations Committee are concerned with the impact of intelligence operations on policy. This has been one of the most frequently reiterated criticisms of the CIA and the intelligence community: that it makes policy, or has too great an influence on policy.

All of the subcommittees concerned with intelligence also desire substantive briefings. This tends to place the Director of Central Intelligence in a difficult position, as the rationale for policy may not always coincide precisely with the National Intelligence Estimate on the same subject. An illustration is the question of whether the Soviet Union is trying to acquire a first-strike capability with its missile system or is simply working toward parity with the United States. At one point this argument reached such proportions that the Foreign Relations Committee had the Secretary of Defense and the Director of Central Intelligence appear together in an attempt to reconcile seemingly conflicting intelligence estimates.

The congressional interest in intelligence is not confined to the above-mentioned subcommittees. Other standing committees have specific interests affecting the intelligence community and its work. The Joint Committee on Atomic Energy, as the parent committee to the Atomic Energy Commission, has a direct interest in the work of that agency's intelligence unit and, further, is concerned with worldwide development in nuclear energy, a subject on which the intelligence agencies are well qualified to report. The Post Office and Civil Service committees are involved and must be consulted on personnel policies, fringe benefits, retirement, and a multitude of other subjects. The Agriculture Committee may request reports on a situation in the Soviet Union that might result in large grain orders. The Committee on the Judiciary is concerned with legal matters: the compiling of dossiers on American citizens. The House Select Committee on Small Business became involved in intelligence operations when it was revealed that certain tax-exempt foundations were being used as conduits for CIA funds. The point can be made that few congressional committees do not have some interest in the work of the intelligence community.

To a degree the courts provide a system of accountability over the intelligence community, although the law gives the CIA considerable freedom of action in the interests of national security. In only rare instances do the intelligence agencies initiate action in the courts. Most cases that reach court are those initiated against them.

Among the first legal actions filed against the CIA, two former employees challenged the authority of the director to terminate the employment of personnel "in the interests of the United States." One case involved an individual who was fired for improper activity. The case had been thoroughly reviewed by the appropriate authorities within the CIA and it had been recommended to the director, the only person empowered to take such action, that the man be fired, which he was. The second case concerned an employee who refused on three occasions to accept assignments that the agency asked him to accept. The CIA's career policy requires that personnel serve where requested. In this instance the employee was allowed to refuse two assignments on the grounds of personal inconvenience. Refusal of the third job offer, which did not involve any great hardship, was considered to be sufficient grounds for dismissal. In both instances the individuals sued the Director of the CIA and in each case the Federal District Court upheld the authority of the head of the agency under the law and handed down summary judgments which were upheld by the Appeals Court.

A considerably more complex case involving an intelligence operation evolved out of what was seemingly a case of alleged slander. In 1964 Eerik Heine, an Estonian émigré resident of Toronto, filed suit against Juri Raus, another former Estonian, alleging that Raus had slandered him by calling him a KGB[12] agent dispatched to North America by the Soviet intelligence service. More than a year passed before there was any indication that the CIA was involved in the case, and only then was there press coverage.

What came to light in the Federal District Court in Baltimore was a brief glimpse of the constant struggle between intelligence services which involved refugees and émigrés. In a 924-page deposition filed with the court, Heine claimed that from 1940 to 1950 he lived in Estonia under constant Soviet persecution. He said he had escaped from prison and managed to reach Canada. During the next decade he became prominent in the affairs of the Legion of Estonian Liberation, one of several hundred organizations of emigrants from the Eastern European countries in the United States and Canada. According to the affidavit, Raus had been

---

[12] The State Security Committee of the Soviet Union: its intelligence and security agency.

responsible for circulating the word among the Estonian refugees that Heine was not an anti-Communist hero but a Soviet agent sent to North America to spy on his fellow countrymen. Raus's initial defense was that it was his privilege to make such a statement as the national commander of the Legion of Estonian Liberation. When this defense did not hold, the true nature of the case emerged.

In the first of four affidavits filed on behalf of the CIA, it was revealed that when Raus had accused Heine of working for the Soviets "he was acting within the scope and course of his employment by the Agency on behalf of the United States." When the judge did not find this affidavit sufficient basis for dismissal of the slander charge against Raus, the CIA filed a second affidavit. This was more explicit:

> For a number of reasons, including his past history and his position as national commander of the Legion of Estonian Liberation, the defendant has been a source to this Agency of foreign intelligence information pertaining interalia to Soviet Estonia and to Estonian émigré activities in foreign countries as well as the United States.

At this point in the trial, the Washington *Post* in its lead editorial on April 22, 1966, under the heading "Above the Law," stated:

> The Central Intelligence Agency is currently engaged in an attempt to deny any means of redress to a man whose character it has ruthlessly assassinated. By open admission of its deputy director, a CIA operative named Juri Raus was instructed to defame an Estonian, Eerik Heine, active in the Estonian Community of the United States by bruiting it about that Mr. Heine was a covert Soviet agent.
> We make no judgment as to the merits of the controversy. . . . But we think it intolerable that government officials

should hold an unlimited license for slander. If, as the CIA asserts, "it would be contrary to the security interests of the United States" to release the information relevant to Mr. Raus' defense, then the CIA ought to indemnify Mr. Heine for the injury done to him. . . .

This case raises some other vital questions. What on earth is the CIA doing trying to manipulate the affairs of the Estonian community in the United States? This kind of interference in the political actions of foreign nationality groups amounts, in our judgment, to a most dangerous sort of subversion, a pollution of one of the main currents of American political life. The CIA ought to be excluded absolutely from involvement in domestic affairs.

Acknowledging that the editorial writer of the *Post* did not have all the facts in the case, or indeed some to be revealed in later testimony, the impassioned commentary made some questionable assumptions: that the CIA was directing one Estonian to make charges against another on other than a basis of solid facts; that the CIA was engaging in "political actions" in foreign nationality groups;[13] that there was, in fact, slander committed. It is interesting to note that this was the last editorial comment by this newspaper on the case.

In an effort to insure justice, the chief judge in the case, Roszel C. Thomsen, insisted that the CIA "go as far as it can go" in supporting Raus in his claim for immunity by giving precisely the instructions the agency had issued. The third affidavit submitted by the CIA described Heine as "a dispatched Soviet intelligence operative, a K.G.B. agent," and elaborated: "The purpose for this instruction was to protect the integrity of the Agency's foreign intelligence sources, existing within or developed through such groups in accordance with the

---

[13] The CIA affidavit, which made it clear that its interest in the Estonian group was foreign intelligence (see above), was submitted to the court on the same day the editorial appeared.

statutory responsibility of the Director of the Central Intelligence Agency to protect foreign intelligence sources and methods. . . ."

Heine then attempted to demonstrate his innocence by inviting arrest when entering the United States from Canada. His counsel attempted to cross-examine Raus, who was directed not to answer questions under a claim of executive privilege by attorneys provided by the government. Heine then invoked Section 16 of Executive Order 10501, under which the President receives and takes action upon complaints from private citizens about the operations of secrecy regulations. The White House reviewed the case but did not intervene.

The Federal District Court ruled for the defendant, Raus, holding that he could not be liable for an alleged slanderous statement made under orders from the CIA. The decision was appealed to the Fourth U.S. Circuit Court of Appeals. Chief Judge Clement F. Haynsworth, Jr., in hearing the case, asked why the CIA did not "leave the defendant to fend for himself," implying that the CIA should never have identified itself with the case and should have let Raus win or lose on the open evidence available. Raus's attorney commented that this might have involved the CIA paying a cash settlement to a person it believed to be an enemy agent. The Circuit Court returned the case to the lower court with the comment: "Absolute privilege is available to Raus if his instructions were issued with the approval of the Director" of the CIA.

If the CIA appeared in court every time its name was invoked to justify some action, criminal or otherwise, the handful of lawyers on the General Counsel's staff of that organization would spend most of their waking hours on the witness stand. The press is usually a co-plaintiff in such cases, as the use of the three letters "CIA" is usually worth a headline. The CIA seldom appears in court unless the Attorney General and the President, as well as the Director of Central Intelligence, believe the appearance necessary in the national interest.

Such a case occurred in the fall of 1966 when three men were charged in the Federal Court for the Western District of New York with taking out of the United States, in violation of the Munitions Control Act, seven Second World War B-26 bombers. It was claimed that the government of Portugal had contracted to buy twenty such aircraft for use against dissident elements in Angola and Mozambique. The U.S. government had told the United Nations that it would not sell military aircraft to Portugal for use in Africa.

The defense counsel in the case contended that the entire venture was a CIA operation and eventually succeeded in having the agency's general counsel testify. The testimony demolished the defense case. The CIA indicated that it was not involved in the case in any manner whatsoever and produced a report from Lisbon dated four days before the first plane was exported that described the entire operation. The CIA report had been circulated to the pertinent agencies in the federal government. Whether the report was not read, or action was taken too late, the export operation avoided detection. In this instance the CIA testimony served to exonerate the U.S. government of any violation of its pledge to the United Nations.

In 1972 the CIA initiated court action to prevent Victor Marchetti, a former employee, from publishing an article describing sensitive operations which he had learned about in the course of his employment. The U.S. District Court for the Eastern District of Virginia granted a permanent injunction against publication of the article which was affirmed by the Fourth Circuit Court of Appeals.

Marchetti had also prepared the outline of a book. The court did not enjoin publication of such a book, but ruled that under the CIA's secrecy agreements, which Marchetti had signed both on entering into CIA employment and when leaving the agency, he was required to submit the manuscript in advance for clearance. The Appeals Court made clear the fact that the CIA could only remove classified information which he had obtained in the course of employment and which was not in the public domain and which the DCI would not approve for release on security grounds. Marchetti's lawyers claimed in their appeal that the requirement for prior clearance was unconstitutional and infringed upon his rights under the First Amendment.

The opinion of the Fourth Circuit Court of Appeals was rendered on September 11, 1972. In it, Chief Judge Clement Haynsworth ruled as follows:

> The question for decision is the enforceability of a secrecy agreement exacted by the government, in its capacity as employer, from an employee of the Central Intelligence Agency. Marchetti contends that his First Amendment rights foreclose any prior restraint upon him in carrying out his purpose to write and publish what he pleases about the Agency and its operations.
>
> We affirm the substance of the decision below, limiting the order, however, to the language of the secrecy agreement Marchetti signed when he joined the Agency.

The pertinent portion of the secrecy agreement is:

> I do solemnly swear that I will never divulge, publish or reveal either by word, conduct, or by any other means, any classified information, intelligence or knowledge except in

the performance of my official duties and in accordance with the laws of the United States, unless specifically authorized in writing, in each case, by the Director of Central Intelligence or his authorized representatives.

The opinion then commented on claims that the CIA oath violated the First Amendment:

Marchetti claims that the present injunction is barred by the Supreme Court decision in the Pentagon Papers case because the Government has failed to meet the very heavy burden against any system of prior restraints on expression. *New York Times Co.* v. *United States*, 403 U.S. 713, 714.

We readily agree with Marchetti that the First Amendment limits the extent to which the United States, contractually or otherwise, may impose secrecy requirements upon its employees and enforce them with a system of prior censorship. It precludes such restraints with respect to information which is unclassified or officially disclosed, but we are here concerned with secret information touching upon the national defense and the conduct of foreign affairs, acquired by Marchetti while in a position of trust and confidence and contractually bound to respect it.

After extensive review of other opinions on freedom of speech, the court commented on the government's right to secrecy.

Gathering intelligence information and the other activities of the Agency, including clandestine affairs against other nations, are all within the President's constitutional responsibility for the security of the Nation as the Chief Executive and as Commander in Chief of our Armed forces. Const., art. II, § 2. Citizens have the right to criticize the conduct of our foreign affairs, but the Government also has the right and the duty to strive for internal secrecy about the conduct of governmental affairs in areas in which disclosure may reasonably be thought to be inconsistent with the national interest.

Although the First Amendment protects criticism of the

government, nothing in the Constitution requires the government to divulge information. . . .

Congress has imposed on the Director of Central Intelligence the responsibility for protecting intelligence sources and methods. 50 U.S.C. § 403 (d) (3). In attempting to comply with this duty, the Agency requires its employees as a condition of employment to sign a secrecy agreement, and such agreements are entirely appropriate to a program in implementation of the congressional direction of secrecy. Marchetti, of course, could have refused to sign, but then he would not have been employed, and he would not have been given access to the classified information he may now want to broadcast.

Moreover, the Government's need for secrecy in this area lends justification to a system of prior restraint against disclosure by employees and former employees of classified information obtained during the course of employment.

As we have said, however, Marchetti by accepting employment with the CIA and by signing a secrecy agreement did not surrender his First Amendment rights of free speech. The agreement is enforceable only because it is not a violation of those rights. We would decline enforcement of the secrecy oath signed when he left the employment of the CIA to the extent that it purports to prevent disclosure of unclassified information, for, to that extent, the oath would be in contravention of his First Amendment rights.

Because we are dealing with a prior restraint upon speech, we think that the CIA must act promptly to approve or disapprove any material which may be submitted to it by Marchetti.

Finally, the opinion commented on judicial review of classified matters:

The Constitution in Article II § 2 confers broad powers upon the President in the conduct of relations with foreign states and in the conduct of the national defense. The CIA is one of the executive agencies whose activities are closely related to the conduct of foreign affairs and to the national defense. Its operations, generally, are an executive function beyond the control of the judicial power. If in the conduct of its operations the need for secrecy requires a system of classification of documents and information, the process of classification is part of the executive function beyond the scope of judicial review.[14]

This case may well become a landmark in establishing a precedent for legal action against intelligence personnel—present and former—who seek to ignore the secrecy oath which all are required to sign. The United States does not have an Official Secrets Act, as does Great Britain, and the result is that some classified information is made public—not just for Americans but for any foreign intelligence service to read or hear. The phenomenon is not new, nor is it confined to any one area of government or level of employment. Also, the motives are varied, ranging from the ambition to appear important, through objection to a given course of action or policy, to personal desire for gain.

[14] *United States of America* v. *Victor L. Marchetti*, U.S. Circuit Court of Appeals for the Fourth Circuit, no. 72–1586.

3

Intelligence and
National Policy

The exact role that intelligence plays in the making of policy, under most circumstances, is difficult to define. There are many considerations aside from intelligence in every important decision made by the President and his advisers. To claim that intelligence determines policy errs on one extreme. To say that intelligence has no influence on presidential determinations is also wrong. Further, the impact that intelligence has on policy will differ on every issue. It cannot be precisely specified.

When the President makes a decision or determines a policy on any issue in the area of national security, he has before him—or he has in mind—the available facts together with the viewpoints and recommendations of the departments and agencies concerned. On occasion, he may invite the leaders of the Congress to the White House and solicit their recommendations, or he may consult by telephone with those Senators or Representatives whose views he respects or whose support he needs. Indeed, he may seek the advice and counsel of distinguished private citizens, as President Kennedy did in the Cuban missile crisis and President Johnson did on Vietnam.

In the modern organization of the Presidency, the key individual in the formulation of policy is the Special Assistant to the President for National Security Affairs, whose role in intelligence was discussed previously. It is his staff that melds the intelligence input with all other policy considerations.

In assembling a policy paper for Presidential action, the contribution from the intelligence community is just one input. Others may come from practically any department or agency in the executive branch and from other sources. The intelligence community is concerned mainly with what other nations have done, are doing, or will do that affects American interests and the other contributions must cover everything else involved. A partial list of the contributions that would be made by the various departments and agencies illustrates the encyclopedic nature of the staff work.

The Department of State is charged with the actual conduct of the foreign relations of the United States. State's jurisdiction and authority have been challenged and infringed upon by a number of other departments and agencies in recent years, but it still is the primary department dealing with the other nations of the world and with international organizations. State's major contribution to a policy paper will deal with the effect of and reaction to the U.S. decision. In preparing its analysis, State may well call on the major agencies that report to the Secretary of State, such as the United States Information Agency which has extensive contacts with foreign news media, the Agency for International Development for an analysis of the economic impact, or the Arms Control and Disarmament Agency if there are matters concerning arms limitation, military assistance, or munitions shipments.

The Defense Department is concerned with many decisions and policies in the national security area. Obviously, if any possible use of military force is involved, Defense becomes a major contributor and must answer such operational questions as whether the ships or planes or men are available or can be made available. Under the Assistant Secretary of Defense for International Security Affairs there exists a miniature State Department. ISA provides the staff work for Defense Department participation on the National Security Council, produces planning studies on political-military areas such as foreign economic affairs and disarmament, supervises the Military Assistance Program, and works on agreements with foreign governments on military facilities, operating rights, and status of forces. A number of policy matters relate to U.S. forces overseas, and Defense, as well as State, must express views on these subjects.

Inasmuch as nearly everything costs money, both the Treasury Department and the Office of Management and Budget are frequent contributors to policy papers. Such questions must be answered as: What will our proposed action do to the federal budget for this or the next fiscal year? Or, what impact will it have on the balance of payments? If major new expenditures are involved, and there may be a pronounced effect on the domestic economy or international trade, the Council of Economic Advisers and the Department of Commerce may be concerned.

Congressional support, or at least neutrality, is a consideration in most policy matters. Except in the most urgent or unusual circumstances, the White House would be reluctant to involve Congress directly in a decision-making process, but indirect assessments will be made of both congressional reaction and public support.

To suggest that each department and agency concerned submit a precise policy or position paper dealing solely with its concerns also is oversimplification. If this were so, the President's staff could assemble all papers, digest and analyze the contents, draw up a list of alternatives, select the most feasible course, and present the President with a neat and complete package.

There are no clear lines of demarcation between policy and intelligence, for example, or between the concerns of State and Defense. A Defense Department paper may include submissions from the Office of the Secretary, from International Security Affairs, from the Joint Chiefs of Staff, and from the Defense Intelligence Agency—to list a few likely contributors. The State Department submission comes principally from area bureaus (about 75 percent), or can come from the Bureau of Intelligence and Research, or other units or individual officials. In fact, on many occasions a senior official may write a policy proposal on his own, or one incorporating several views. In most such papers intelligence assessments will be included, directly quoting a National Intelligence Estimate, or a senior officer may submit his personal intelligence estimate of the situation.

One modern case history of the role of intelligence in decision-making is the Cuban missile crisis of October 1962. Although this confrontation between the United States and Russia has been analyzed from many points of view and has been the subject of one or two brilliant studies,[1] some emphasis on the intelligence aspects are

[1] At the time of the crisis, Roger Hilsman was Director of the Bureau of Intelligence and Research of the State Department. A graduate of West Point, with a doctorate in political science from Yale, Hilsman fought with Merrill's Marauders and an OSS guerrilla team in Burma in the Second World War, was Assistant Secretary of State for Far Eastern Affairs (1963), and then professor in the Columbia University School of International Affairs. The three chapters in his *To Move a Nation* (Garden City, N.Y.: Doubleday, 1967) dealing with the Cuban missile crisis constitute an incisive analysis of intelligence and the policy-making process.

Of the major participants, Robert F. Kennedy, the Attorney General, and brother, and closest confidant of the President, in a book published after the author's death, *Thirteen Days: A Memoir of the Cuban Missile Crisis* (New York: Norton, 1969), provides an intimate and moving reflection of the deep personal and emotional involvement of President Kennedy in the greatest crisis

worthwhile. Not only does this episode provide striking illustrations of what intelligence can and cannot produce, it is almost a model for the meshing of intelligence and policy at every step of the decision-making process. The missile crisis was a confrontation of utmost gravity of the two superpowers, and the future of the world depended on the accuracy of the information available to each and the quality of their analysis.

President Kennedy emphasized the latter point in his message to Khrushchev of October 22, when he said: ". . . The one thing that has most concerned me has been the possibility that your government would not correctly understand the will and determination of the United States in any given situation. . . ." [2] The President was reflecting the most difficult of all subjects for intelligence to discover, the national will, and he was terribly concerned that the Russians might underestimate American resolution.

Robert McNamara made this comment: "The performance of the U.S. Government during that critical period was more effective than at any other time during my seven years as Secretary of Defense. The agencies of the Government: the State Department, the civilian and military leaders of the Defense Department, the CIA, the

---

of his administration. The last two chapters, "Some of the things we learned . . ." and "The importance of placing ourselves in the other country's shoes," are most important for those who would understand the role of intelligence in the policy process.

Another who sat with the so-called Executive Committee of the National Security Council, Special Counsel Theodore C. Sorensen, in his book *Kennedy* (New York: Harper & Row, 1965), devoted a chapter to the missile crisis. Historian Arthur M. Schlesinger, Jr., who was in the White House at the time but did not actively participate in the Executive Committee meetings, wrote about it in *A Thousand Days: John F. Kennedy in the White House* (Boston: Houghton Mifflin, 1965). A distinguished journalist, Elie Abel, wrote a day-by-day account in *The Missile Crisis* (Philadelphia: Lippincott, 1966).

[2] *Thirteen Days*, p. 79.

White House staff, the U.N. mission, worked together smoothly and harmoniously." [3]

The crisis did not originate solely from the introduction of Russian offensive weapons into Cuba; it had been building for two years. John F. Kennedy, in his campaign for the Presidency in 1960, made strong attacks on the Republicans for their handling of Castro and Cuba. He inherited an operation to overthrow Castro and was deeply shocked by the failure at the Bay of Pigs less than ninety days after he took office. He admitted to Khrushchev at Vienna in June 1961 that the operation had been a mistake, to which Khrushchev replied that the attempted landing had only increased Cuba's fears that the Americans would impose another Batista. Khrushchev also told Kennedy that Castro was not a Communist but that U.S. policy could make him one.[4]

In the summer of 1962, the intelligence community followed developments in Cuba most carefully. Two estimates were produced. The first, in August, dealt with Cuban affairs generally but, inter alia, concluded in effect that the Russians would not put offensive weapons on the island. The second, which was concerned almost entirely with the question of offensive weapons and which reached the same conclusion, was dated September 19. By that time there was substantial worry in Washington about the arms buildup, and the intelligence agencies stressed in their paper that a most careful watch must be kept on the situation. A briefing at the State Department and three separate comments by the President had alerted the American public, the Cubans, the Russians, and the world to the fact that the United States was deeply concerned by what was going on in Cuba.

The September 19, 1962, National Intelligence Esti-

---

[3] In the introduction to Robert Kennedy's *Thirteen Days*, p. 14.
[4] Sorensen, *Kennedy*, p. 546.

mate became a *cause célèbre* because it continued to express the conviction that the Russians would not put offensive weapons in Cuba. Why? Because on that date there was no conclusive evidence of any such weapons there, and a major collection effort was being made to learn the facts. There was hard intelligence on SAM sites (surface-to-air missiles), coastal defense positions, old model Soviet MIG aircraft, missile patrol boats, and Soviet technicians, but nothing on offensive weapons that could pose a serious threat to the United States. There had been a flood of reports from Cuban refugees on Soviet missiles in Cuba. Many of these reports conflicted with one another or were obviously inaccurate. In any case, each such report had to be checked with great care, as the émigrés wanted nothing so much as a U.S. invasion to overthrow Castro. Members of Congress used the refugee reports to challenge the administration, claiming that key "facts" were being ignored, thus making it a dominant issue in the congressional elections.

Without any hard evidence concerning offensive weapons, the intelligence community had to "estimate" on the basis of prior Russian performance. The Soviets previously had put each of the weapons systems known to be in Cuba in other countries. They had never given offensive missiles to other nations; nor had they ever before, or since, displayed a willingness to proceed with ventures that would so clearly and significantly raise the level of risk in U.S.–Soviet relations. The Russians presumably knew that offensive weapons in Cuba would bring a prompt and perhaps violent American reaction. The estimators did not, perhaps could not, foresee that the Russians would badly miscalculate on this score. That, in brief, was the reasoning of the intelligence experts.

There was one official with grave doubts about the

accuracy of the intelligence estimate. This was John A. McCone, the Director of Central Intelligence. He could not see the logic of the elaborate and expensive SAM and radar sites for defensive purposes alone. He expressed his concern to Robert Kennedy, Dean Rusk, Robert McNamara, and McGeorge Bundy, and he put great pressure on the intelligence system to dig harder for the facts, but he acknowledged that the hard evidence was missing and allowed the estimate to go forward. As Director of Central Intelligence, the National Intelligence Estimate was his. McCone could have changed it to read that "it appeared likely that the Soviets would put offensive weapons in Cuba" and forced all of the other intelligence chiefs to dissent, if they chose to do so.

President Kennedy was asked at his news conference on August 29 about the reports concerning Russian missiles in Cuba. He replied: "We cannot base the issue of war and peace on a rumor or report which is not substantial, or which some member of Congress refuses to tell us where he heard it. To persuade our allies to come to us, to hazard the security . . . as well as the peace of the free world, we have to move with hard intelligence." [5]

It was against this background that such senior officials as Under Secretary of State George W. Ball (to a congressional committee) and Special Assistant to the President McGeorge Bundy (on the American Broadcasting Company's program "Issues and Answers") continued to state in early October 1962 that the weapons in Cuba were of a defensive nature.

On October 15, U-2 photography revealed for the first time evidence of preparation for a medium-range ballistic missile site near San Cristobal in western Cuba. Erectors,

[5] Quoted in *ibid.*, p. 670.

transporters, and missile-ready tents, identical to those on sites photographed in Russia by U-2's, had been moved into position. It is interesting to note that even though the photo-interpreter considered this conclusive proof, the average layman (or even sophisticated government officials) did not see it as such. Robert Kennedy said: ". . . What I saw appeared to be no more than the clearing of a field for a farm or the basement of a house. I was relieved to hear later that this was the same reaction of virtually everyone at the meeting, including President Kennedy. Even a few days later, when more work had taken place on the site, he remarked that it looked like a football field." [6]

The explanations of the experts in photo-interpretation, plus corroborative evidence, convinced the President and his principal advisers that the Russians were indeed installing missiles with nuclear warheads which could strike the United States. From such a short distance away there would be little or no advance warning. In retrospect, it seems that if the photographs were initially viewed with skepticism, unconfirmed agent or refugee reports would have been even less convincing.

After seeing the photographs and accepting the evidence as conclusive, President Kennedy's first action was to establish an advisory group, including the Director of Central Intelligence and the principals of State and Defense. Perhaps even more important, this group, which became known as the "ExComm" (for Executive Committee of the National Security Council), represented men whose wisdom the President respected. The President was not seeking standard departmental viewpoints or a packaged solution. He directed that every alternative be explored from living with the missiles, on one extreme,

[6] *Thirteen Days*, p. 24.

to destroying the sites by surprise attack, on the other. He wanted the discussions to be free, intent, and continuous, with views expressed regardless of an individual's hierarchical position or a department's policy.

The President wanted a variety of views and suggestions as to courses of action so he could weigh alternatives. He so constituted the ExComm that he would receive not only the estimates of the intelligence community—through the Director of Central Intelligence and the Chairman of the Joint Chiefs of Staff (frequently accompanied by the Director of the Defense Intelligence Agency)—but also the analyses of such experts as former ambassadors to Moscow (Bohlen and Thompson), the Assistant Secretary of State for Latin America, and others.

Keeping in mind that the objective was to persuade the Soviet Union to remove its missile sites from Cuba, review of the questions posed shows not only how much the answers depended on correct information and accurate analysis but also that intelligence and policy are frequently inextricable.

On the first day of meetings (Tuesday, October 16), the President directed that increased U-2 reconnaissance flights be undertaken and that aircraft be readied for low-level flights to be flown when authorized. The photographs from these flights would give even more detailed information than those from the high-altitude U-2. Robert Kennedy says in *Thirteen Days* that the film for one day during the crisis was twenty-five miles long.[7] The President held off on low-level flights in order not to alert the Russians that the United States was now aware of the missile sites and was making a major effort to observe the construction. It had been assumed that the

[7] P. 68.

Russians in Cuba were aware of the U-2 flights and thus must have deduced that the Americans were watching the construction. As mentioned above, official statements from Washington expressed concern about Russian weapons in Cuba. What would the Soviet leaders do in this complex game of one nation signaling the other? Would they ignore the signal and believe they could proceed with impunity to complete the sites?

One thing seemed certain. The Russians must understand that the United States knew what was going on. Of course, this assumed that the Russians in Cuba advised Moscow of the U-2 flights, that Russian intelligence knew of the quality of U.S. aerial photography (they had shot down the U-2 on May 1, 1960, and had seen its camera), and that the Americans would be able to determine what was being built. Could U.S. intelligence make these assumptions about the Russians with certainty?

Also on the first day, President Kennedy directed that the ExComm work in the utmost secrecy so as not to alert the Russians to the possibility of reprisal until the United States decided on its course of action. How did this reconcile with the low-level flights? The reconnaissance was necessary, but the indication of a major crisis involving the President was another matter. If it became known that the ExComm was in almost continual session, the Washington press corps could generate enough pressure to force a government statement. Just daily headlines on the ExComm meetings would stimulate enough congressional interest and public anxiety to require a presidential announcement. Not much imagination is needed to envisage the headline: "Top Defense and State Officials in Continuous Sessions." "President Refuses to Disclose Subject of Discussion." The President also assumed, and rightly, that once the press was aware of a crisis it would not be long before the locale of the crisis was identified. He wanted to be able to decide on a course of action without the added domestic pressures to what was already the great burden of a major international crisis.

Finally, on the first day, the alternative actions discussed were an air strike to destroy the missile sites versus acquiescence. The Soviet experts in ExComm said Moscow's reaction would be unpredictable as to an air strike that would kill Russians. Latin American experts observed that Cubans would be killed and that the United States would suffer in the hemisphere. The authorities on Europe were concerned that the American reaction would be regarded as excessive and, together with the Kremlinologists, worried about the Russians taking countermeasures affecting Berlin. In the discussion of acquiescence, the two major analyses concerned whether the Russians would interpret this as a sign of weakness and become even more aggressive and how no action would be viewed in the rest of the world. One could argue that all of these questions were strictly for intelligence. However, all participants in ExComm had strong views on each.

On the second day (Wednesday, October 17), the principal subject of discussion was a naval blockade. Again the major question was: How would the Russians react? The third day one important item was concerned with how the Russians could retreat with dignity.

In thirteen days the chief decision-makers of the government reviewed a virtual encyclopedia of action-reaction possibilities involving not just what Russia would do and how the United States would react, and vice versa, but what the reactions of many other nations would be.[8] A study was made of possible Soviet reaction

[8] Sorensen in *Kennedy* has an excellent chapter on the crisis, "The

against Berlin, already the scene of a serious confrontation between the United States and Russia, or against the American Jupiter missiles in Turkey and Iran. The support of the Organization of American States was considered important to the "legalistic-minded decision-makers in the Kremlin," according to former Ambassador Llewellyn Thompson. The President asked Secretary of State Rusk to prepare a list of all possible allied reactions, which was presented to ExComm on the second day.

To complicate the deliberations of the ExComm, the Soviet Union, as the record now quite clearly indicates, was engaged in a deception plan. The best that can be said for them is that they did not intend to admit that there were missiles in Cuba until the sites were operational and could be used to force major concessions from the United States. Perhaps Khrushchev was counting not only on lack of resolve by President Kennedy but may have been influenced by the President's obvious disillusionment with the CIA and the intelligence community after the Bay of Pigs, which might cause him to reject their reports on Cuba.

The deception plan called for continuous and repeated assertions by Soviet officials that no weapons that could threaten the United States would be put in Cuba. On August 23 Theodore Sorensen, the Special Counsel to the President, had called on Soviet Ambassador Anatoly F. Dobrynin to advise him that the congressional elections would not inhibit American reactions to any new pressures on Berlin. On September 6 Dobrynin called Sorensen to the embassy on an urgent basis and read him the reply from Moscow:

> Nothing will be undertaken before the American Congressional elections that could complicate the international

Confrontation in Cuba," and on page 680 and elsewhere lists the questions considered.

situation or aggravate the tension in the relations between our two countries . . . provided there are no actions taken on the other side which would change the situation.[9]

George Bolshakov, an embassy official in Washington, told his American contacts that both Khrushchev and Mikoyan had told him no missile capable of reaching the United States would be placed in Cuba.[10] On Thursday, October 18, when the United States had conclusive photographic proof of the missile bases, Soviet Foreign Minister Andrei Gromyko, in a two-hour meeting with President Kennedy, read from notes:

> As to Soviet assistance to Cuba, I have been instructed to make it clear, as the Soviet Government has already done, that such assistance pursued solely the purpose of contributing to the defense capabilities of Cuba and to the development of its peaceful economy . . . training by Soviet specialists of Cuban nationals in handling defensive armaments was by no means offensive. If it were otherwise, the Soviet Government would have never become involved in rendering such assistance.[11]

On October 16 Foy Kohler, the new U.S. Ambassador to the Soviet Union, had been received by Khrushchev, who said he wanted to state once again that all activity in Cuba was defensive.[12] When Ambassador Adlai Stevenson showed the UN Security Council photographs of the missile sites, the Soviet representative Zorin charged that the CIA had manufactured the evidence.

The purpose of this duplicity, not unique in world history, was to mislead as to Soviet intentions: to neutralize U.S. intelligence collection and pose greater difficulties for the American decision-makers.

[9] *Ibid.*, p. 667.
[10] *Ibid.*, p. 668.
[11] *Ibid.*, p. 690.
[12] *Ibid.*, p. 691.

In the course of the Cuban missile crisis, President Kennedy's concern with intelligence operations was greater than usual. He kept tight control on reconnaissance flights and was greatly concerned when thousands of miles from the crisis area a plane strayed over Soviet territory. He told the Navy to move a communications intelligence ship away from Cuba so as not to provoke an incident. The President also restricted the circulation of reports on the missile sites within the government to lessen the chances of leaks.

The intelligence community operated on a twenty-four-hour-day basis during the crisis. Starting on August 27, a daily situation report on Cuba was circulated to top federal officials. On October 16 the USIB commenced daily meetings to approve national estimates for presentation to the ExComm at its morning meeting. The photo-interpreters, who already had been working extra shifts, put in exhausting hours to cope with the miles of film arriving each day. Every agency's collectors, especially the CIA's, watched Soviet activity throughout the world, with particular concentration on crisis spots such as Berlin, Turkey, and Iran. Not only were all moves by Russian diplomats studied but those of Soviet intelligence personnel were followed even more intently than usual (if that was possible).

At the height of the crisis, the Russians used the KGB *Rezident* in Washington (their intelligence station chief), Aleksandr Fomin, to contact John Scali, an ABC–TV correspondent covering the State Department, to ascertain "unofficially" U.S. intentions. Scali immediately advised the State Department and was given the official American position, as communicated to Moscow, to give to Fomin. There was valuable guidance in this action for U.S. intelligence. It was apparent that the Russians wanted confirmation of the U.S. position from other than conventional channels. Even the demeanor of Fomin was instructive: Scali reported his nervousness and the fact that he paid for a thirty-cent check for coffee with a five-dollar bill and didn't wait for the change.

That the intelligence community acquitted itself well in the Cuban missile crisis should be evident from the result. Perhaps as important was the restoration of the President's confidence in intelligence. Not long after the end of the crisis he was asked by one of his assistants to autograph a portrait to hang in the conference room of the CIA. He wrote: "To the CIA—with esteem." Another aide, observing this, is reported to have said, "Sir, if you do that for CIA you will have to do it for all of the other departments and agencies." The President is reported to have replied, "Maybe I don't hold them all in esteem." Key elements of the intelligence community—the photo-interpreters, aerial-reconnaissance units, and others—received Presidential citations.

Quite a different perspective on the impact of intelligence on policy is given by a look at that portion of the official record of the Vietnam War now available. In August 1954 the U.S. government, strongly influenced by Secretary of State John Foster Dulles, who viewed the Geneva accords on Indochina as a major catastrophe opening South Asia to Communism, decided on direct military and economic aid to South Vietnam. A National Intelligence Estimate calculated the prospects of success:

> Although it is possible that the French and Vietnamese, even with firm support from the U.S. and other powers, may be able to establish a strong regime in South Vietnam, we believe that the chances for this development are poor and moreover, that the situation is more likely to continue to deteriorate progressively over the next year.[13]

[13] Neil Sheehan and E. W. Kenworthy, eds., *The Pentagon Papers* (New York: Quadrangle, 1972), p. 7.

The Pentagon Papers noted that the intelligence community was skeptical of success in Indochina:

> Intelligence analysts in the Central Intelligence Agency, the State Department and sometimes the Pentagon repeatedly warned that the French, Emperor Bao Dai and Premier Diem were weak and unpopular and that the Communists were strong.[14]

Why then into the quagmire? In 1954 there were many reasons. To the Secretary of State, battling the Communists was the quest for the holy grail. The Geneva Accords had given the Communists North Vietnam. They must be stopped from taking the South. The Republicans had accused the Democrats of "losing China," and now, in their turn, they didn't want to lose Indochina. Further, the United States could succeed where France had failed. America had limitless power and a demonstration of U.S. support could overawe the Vietnamese Communists into quitting.

Even though the Secretary of State's brother was the Director of Central Intelligence, there may well have been a tendency not to give the pessimistic view of the intelligence estimates too much weight. The CIA and the intelligence community were less than seven years old. President Eisenhower, as military commander, had had ample experience with faulty and overly pessimistic intelligence. The Secretary of State was confident of the course of action to follow. The President accepted his judgment.

In the years following the 1954 American decision to assist South Vietnam, there were many problems for the intelligence agencies, but the two major concerns were: What were the Communists doing, and what was hap-

[14] *Ibid.*, p. 7.

pening in President Diem's government? Both were covered reasonably well. An estimate of May 1959 gave a precise view of Diem and his government, using such phrases as "undisputed ruler," "façade of representative government," "authoritarian," "no organized opposition, loyal or otherwise, is tolerated," and commented on programs that resulted in less rather than more security.[15]

The intelligence agencies were not so preoccupied with the stability of the government in Saigon that external threats were ignored. Early in 1959, the CIA reported increased infiltration from the north by special border-crossing teams operating under a 559th Transportation Group directly controlled by the party's Central Committee. Most of the infiltrators were Southerners who had gone north in 1954 at the time of the division of the country. Training centers for infiltrators were reported at Xuanmai and Sontay. During 1959 and 1960, intelligence reports said twenty-six groups totaling 4,500 persons were infiltrated.[16]

In August 1960 an estimate concluded: "The indications of increasing dissatisfaction with the Diem government have probably encouraged the Hanoi regime to take stronger action at this time." [17]

By the fall of 1961 the increase in guerrilla activity in the South reached such proportions that President Diem was putting pressure on the U.S. government for a bilateral defense treaty and an increased American military buildup. The Joint Chiefs of Staff proposed that the United States seize and hold major areas in Laos. Others proposed putting American combat troops in Vietnam. The intelligence community was now emphasizing the indigenous nature of the uprising. A Special

[15] For more extensive quotations, see *ibid.*, pp. 73–74.
[16] *Ibid.*, p. 80.
[17] *Ibid.*, p. 73.

National Intelligence Estimate on October 5, 1961, said "that 80–90 per cent of the estimated 17,000 VC [in South Vietnam] had been locally recruited, and that there was little evidence that the VC relied on external supplies." The estimate commented on the high quality and staying power of the VC against any intervention.[18]

That month President Kennedy sent his military adviser, General Maxwell Taylor, to South Vietnam for an independent assessment. General Taylor advised providing a "U.S. military presence capable of raising national morale and of showing to Southeast Asia the seriousness of the U.S. intent to resist a Communist take-over." [19] A Special National Intelligence Estimate of November 5 said that the North Vietnamese would respond to an increased U.S. commitment with an offsetting commitment of their own: the greater the American involvement, the stronger the North Vietnamese reaction.[20]

By 1963 there was public optimism being expressed by American officials about the guerrilla situation in South Vietnam. But an estimate of April 17, 1963, described the situation as fragile and said there was no persuasive evidence that the enemy had been seriously hurt.[21]

A Special National Intelligence Estimate 53-2-63, "The Situation in South Vietnam," dated July 10, 1963, analyzing the Buddhist crisis, said, "Disorders will probably flare again and the chances of a coup or assassination attempts against him (Diem) will become better than ever." [22] The accuracy of the estimate was not long in being realized. To quote Hedrick Smith's analysis of the Pentagon Papers for this period: "Washington did not

[18] *Ibid.*, p. 103.
[19] *Ibid.*, p. 108.
[20] *Ibid.*, p. 110.
[21] *Ibid.*, p. 170.
[22] *Ibid.*, Doc. 34, p. 199.

originate the anti-Diem coup, nor did American forces intervene in any way. . . . But for weeks—and with the White House informed every step of the way—the American mission in Saigon maintained secret contacts with the plotting generals through one of the Central Intelligence Agency's most experienced and versatile operatives. . . ." [23] The documents now available to the public reveal the extent to which the intelligence agency was used as liaison with the dissident group that overthrew Diem on November 3, 1963.

By 1964 the continued increase in guerrilla activity in the South led Washington to consider stronger action against the North to force Hanoi to reduce or stop its support of the Vietcong. President Johnson in a directive for contingency planning said: "Particular attention should be given to shaping such pressures so as to produce the maximum credible deterrent effect on Hanoi." [24] The intelligence community said, "The primary sources of Communist strength in South Vietnam are indigenous," but various policy-makers were convinced that a threat to bomb the industry in the North would force concessions from Ho Chi Minh, who had gone to such efforts to rebuild the country.[25] In effect, this was to remain the key difference between the intelligence community and the policy-makers: the former skeptical about bombing breaking the will of the North; the latter convinced it would force concessions. This was not the only action considered, however. Every possibility was considered, including U.S. withdrawal.

In June 1964 President Johnson asked the CIA: "Would the rest of Southeast Asia necessarily fall if Laos and South Vietnam came under North Vietnamese con-

[23] *Ibid.*, p. 167.
[24] *Ibid.*, p. 249.
[25] *Ibid.*, pp. 249–50.

trol?" The reply of June 9 stated: "With the possible exception of Cambodia, it is likely that no nation in the area would quickly succumb to Communism as a result of the fall of Laos and South Vietnam. Furthermore, a continuation of the spread of Communism in the area would not be inexorable, and any spread which did occur would take time—time in which the total situation might change in any number of ways unfavorable to the Communist cause." But the estimate indicated the loss of those two countries would be a serious blow to the position of the United States in the Far East.[26]

In November 1964 three plans for action against North Vietnam were under consideration in Washington, ranging from reprisals or tit-for-tat through progressive escalation to an intensive bombardment, until U.S. terms were met. An intelligence panel composed of representatives of the CIA, the DIA, and State's Bureau of Intelligence and Research did not see any strong likelihood of breaking Hanoi's will.[27] Perhaps even more important was a most prophetic comment: ". . . In any event comprehension of the other's intentions would almost certainly be difficult on both sides, and especially as the scale of hostilities mounted." [28] In more blunt terms, what intelligence was saying to the policy-makers was: We don't believe military action will break Hanoi. We admit it is hard to judge their intentions. It is hard for them to judge our intentions. As the war gets hotter, it is going to be even harder for both sides to judge the other. In retrospect, maybe intelligence did not place enough emphasis on this view. There is always a tendency for decision-makers to think the other side will react rationally, logically—and the way we expect them to. On the

[26] *Ibid.*, p. 262.
[27] *Ibid.*, p. 340.
[28] *Ibid.*, p. 340.

other hand, there is a limit to how far the intelligence community can stress a point.

Before the sustained bombing of the North (Operation Rolling Thunder, launched on March 2, 1965) could have any major effect on the guerrilla war in the South, there were indications that the Saigon war effort was in danger of collapse and a decision was made to commit American ground troops. The debate among the policy-makers was in many respects similar to that on bombing: How much and in what intensity? As with the air attack, there was skepticism.

On April 2, 1965, the Director of Central Intelligence, John A. McCone, who had already resigned and was soon to be replaced, circulated a memorandum to the Secretaries of State and Defense, the Special Assistant to the President, and Ambassador Taylor. McCone commented on the proposal discussed the previous day to commit ground forces to active combat accompanied by a slowly ascending tempo of bombing operations. He suggested that committing ground troops would be effective only if accompanied by bombing "sufficiently heavy and damaging to really hurt the North Vietnamese," otherwise the North would believe the United States was still temporizing. He went on to say: "I have reported that the strikes to date have not caused a change in the North Vietnamese policy of directing Viet Cong insurgency, infiltrating cadres and supplying material. If anything, the strikes to date have hardened their attitude."

McCone went on to predict both American public reaction against the war and forecast the course of the war with remarkable accuracy.

On the other hand, we must look with care to our position under a program of slowly ascending tempo of air strikes. With the passage of each day and each week, we can expect increasing pressure to stop the bombing. This will come from various elements of the American public, from the press, the United Nations and world opinion. Therefore time will run against us in this operation and I think the North Vietnamese are counting on this.

Therefore I think what we are doing is starting on a track which involves ground force operations, which, in all probability, will have limited effectiveness against guerrillas, although admittedly will restrain some VC advances. However, we can expect requirements for an ever-increasing commitment of U.S. personnel without materially improving the chances of victory. . . .[29]

McCone, probably not certain that Special Assistant McGeorge Bundy had shown his paper to the President, sent a personal memorandum to Mr. Johnson on April 28 expressing the same views. A special intelligence estimate of May 8 from Vice Admiral William F. Raborn, McCone's successor as Director of Central Intelligence, repeated these arguments.

In the summer of 1965 the objective of the air attack against the North was changed. It was no longer an effort to break the will of North Vietnam but to cut the flow of men and supplies to the South. A DIA analysis of the bombing results, requested by Secretary McNamara, made the following statements:

The air strikes do not appear to have altered Hanoi's determination to continue supporting the war in Vietnam.

The idea that destroying, or threatening to destroy, North Vietnam's industry would pressure Hanoi into calling it quits, seems, in retrospect, a colossal misjudgment.[30]

In November of 1965 Secretary McNamara asked the CIA what the effect would be of bombing North Vietnam's oil tank farms. The reply stated:

[29] Mike Gravel, ed., *The Senator Gravel Edition—The Pentagon Papers* (Boston: Beacon Press, 1971), III, Doc. 91, p. 450.
[30] Sheehan and Kenworthy, *The Pentagon Papers*, p. 480.

It is unlikely that this loss would cripple the Communist military operations in the South, though it would certainly embarrass them.

We do not believe that the attacks in themselves would lead to a major change of policy on the Communist side, either toward negotiations or toward enlarging the war.

The Secretary of Defense asked what would happen if the United States bombed all major targets in North Vietnam. The CIA replied: "The D.R.V. would not decide to quit; P.A.V.N. infiltration South would continue." [31]

On January 24, 1966, Secretary McNamara wrote a memorandum to the President in which he recommended increasing the bombing strikes against North Vietnam and raising the number of U.S. troops in the South to more than 400,000. His memorandum read in part:

Deployments of the kind we have recommended will not guarantee success. Our intelligence estimate is that the present Communist policy is to continue to prosecute the war vigorously in the South. They continue to believe that the war will be a long one, that time is their ally, and that their staying power is superior to ours. They recognize that the U.S. reinforcements of 1965 signify a determination to avoid defeat, and that more U.S. troops can be expected. Even though the Communists will continue to suffer heavily from GVN and U.S. ground and air action, we expect them, upon learning of any U.S. intentions to augment its forces, to boost their own commitment and to test U.S. capabilities and will to persevere at higher level of conflict and casualties. . . .[32]

McNamara in this instance was paraphrasing an intelligence estimate of December 3, 1965.[33]

[31] *Ibid.*, pp. 487–88.
[32] *Ibid.*, Doc. 108, pp. 500–02.
[33] *Ibid.*, p. 488.

In the summer of 1966, the Institute of Defense Analysis convened a panel of forty-seven scientists described as "the cream of the scholarly community in technical fields." Their report emphasized the conclusions of the intelligence agencies that the bombing had had "no measurable effect." [34]

The intelligence community's views on the effect of bombing on North Vietnam changed remarkably little throughout the years, even though it was obvious that such conclusions were not popular with the top officials. In May 1967 the CIA submitted three papers. One concluded that twenty-seven months of bombing "have had remarkably little effect on Hanoi's over-all strategy in prosecuting the war, on its confident view of long-term Communist prospects, and on its political tactics regarding negotiations." The second paper assessed the attitude in North Vietnam as "resolute stoicism with a considerable reservoir of endurance still untapped." The third reported the view that losses from the bombings had not resulted in any meaningful loss of ability to continue the war in the South.[35]

Four years later this estimate still held. The first National Security Study Memorandum (NSSM)[36] requested by the Nixon administration in January 1969, an analysis of the situation in Vietnam prepared by the staff of the Special Assistant to the President for National Security Affairs on the basis of studies prepared in State, Defense, and CIA said: "MACV/JCS (the Military Assistance Command, Vietnam in Saigon, and the Joint Chiefs of Staff in Washington) believe that a vigorous

[34] *Ibid.*, p. 473.
[35] *Ibid.*, p. 547.
[36] NSSM-1 was introduced into the Congressional Record by Representative Ronald V. Dellums on May 10, 1972, and is published on that date and May 11, 1972, on pages E 4975–5005 and 5009–5048.

bombing campaign could choke off enough supplies to Hanoi to make her stop fighting, while OSD (the Office of the Secretary of Defense in Washington) and CIA see North Vietnam continuing the struggle against unlimited bombing." [37]

NSSM-1 analyzed why there were differences in the U.S. government on intelligence appraisals:

> The responses to the questions posed regarding Vietnam show agreement on some matters as well as very substantial differences of opinion within the U.S. government on many aspects of the Vietnam situation. While there are some divergencies on the facts, the sharpest differences arise in the interpretation of those facts, the relative weight to be given them, and the implications to be drawn. In addition, there remain certain areas where our information remains inadequate.

The study goes on to identify the differences by organization, divided roughly into two major groups.

> The first school, which we will call Group A, usually includes MACV, CINCPAC (Commander In Chief, Pacific), JCS and Embassy, Saigon, and takes a hopeful view of current and future prospects in Vietnam. . . . The second school, Group B, usually includes OSD, CIA and (to a lesser extent) State and is decidedly more skeptical about the present and pessimistic about the future. There are, of course, disagreements within agencies across the board on specific issues.
>
> In explaining reduced enemy military presence and activities, Group A gives greater relative weight to allied military pressure, than does Group B.
>
> The improvements in RVNAF (Republic of Vietnam Armed Forces) are considered much more significant by Group A than Group B.
>
> Group A underlines advancements in the pacification program, while Group B is skeptical both of the evaluation

[37] NSSM-1, E 4981.

system used to measure progress and of the solidity of recent advances.

In looking at the political scene, Group A accents recent improvements while Group B highlights remaining obstacles and strengths of the NLF (National Liberation Front).

Group A assigns much greater effectiveness to the bombing in Vietnam and Laos than Group B.[38]

In commenting on a National Intelligence Estimate on the speed of the "domino theory," NSSM-1 refers to ". . . major disagreements within the same Department. Within the Defense Department, OSD and DIA support the conclusions of the NIE, while Army, Navy and Air Force Intelligence dissent. Within State, the Bureau of Intelligence supports the NIE while the East Asian Bureau dissents." [39]

One conclusion drawn by the study is: "It is noteworthy that the gap in views that does exist is largely one between the policy makers, the analysts, and the intelligence community on one hand, and the civilian and military operators on the other." [40]

While the above conclusion might be valid for the views submitted in January 1969 on the situation in Vietnam, the record produced in the Pentagon Papers seldom places the policy-makers and the intelligence community on the same side. The intelligence community was consistently skeptical about the efficacy of the measures attempted to end the conflict in Vietnam and pessimistic about the results. Unfortunately, there is no evidence that the men making the decisions and those providing the intelligence ever met together and hammered out the differences, as was done in the SALT talks.

Can either the Vietnam War or the Cuban missile crisis

[38] *Ibid.*, E 4977.
[39] *Ibid.*, E 4978.
[40] *Ibid.*, E 4980.

be considered typical of the role of the intelligence community in the formulation of policy? In the missile crisis President Kennedy established a new group to advise him, the so-called Executive Committee of the National Security Council—unique at the time and unduplicated since. The ExComm enabled extensive examination and discussion of intelligence reports by policy-makers and afforded an exchange with the intelligence community which was an important factor in the working of the system. In the missile crisis, hard intelligence was available on what had happened and was happening. The unknown factor was how the Soviet Union would react when asked to remove the missiles or face the possibility that the United States would destroy the sites. The 1962 crisis was of short duration, and from the American point of view was resolved with minimum loss.

The Vietnam War has been far more complex, prolonged—extending over four administrations—and frustrating to the policy-makers. The role, and even the credibility of the intelligence community, differed in each administration. The style of each President and the environment of decision-making varied considerably. While the concerned officials met together frequently, there was no real continuity as even the career civil servants and foreign service officers were reassigned or left the government. Those disagreeing with the policy or actions taken were deliberately excluded from the meetings where decisions were being made. It was very much an *ad hoc* affair. The unanswered (and perhaps unanswerable) questions facing the intelligence community were many: What would it take to force Hanoi to negotiate? What would China and the Soviet Union do under a variety of circumstances? What was the durability of South Vietnam? —to mention only a few. Perhaps most important to the policy-makers was a question beyond the ken of the intelligence community: What was the will of the American people?

The two case studies serve to emphasize the major problems confronting the intelligence community.

1. Hard intelligence seldom, if ever, exists in the quantity or quality needed. There are and always will be gaps in information not just on such critical issues as what the Russians might do over Cuba or the Communists in Vietnam but on subjects of much less secrecy and consequence. Policy-makers frequently voice their disappointment that the intelligence community did not predict a coup in advance or forecast the results of an election. Sherman Kent, former Yale historian and for many years the Assistant Director of the CIA responsible for national estimates, expressed what became known as the "Kent Law of Coups," which was simply: Those coups that are known about in advance don't take place. As long as unexpected political alignments take place, as long as governments change policies without prior announcement, as long as men act irrationally, and as long as there are national secrets, even the best intelligence service in the world will not be able to keep fully informed.

2. The problem of interpretation of information is most difficult. Assuming that every individual in the intelligence process has all of the information available, there still may be many variations of interpretation, perhaps as many as the number of individuals concerned. Add to this a natural instinct to think of one's own service interests first; disputes over an estimate then become inevitable. When the estimate reaches the policy level, it may be received with varied reactions.

National Intelligence Estimates can be studied only in

the context of the world situation at the time of preparation. Partial quotations from summaries of NIE's used to emphasize a point may ignore phrases in other portions of the estimate that tend to qualify the conclusion. If modifying phrases fit more closely to the views of one or more of the policy-makers, such conclusions are likely to be emphasized to the exclusion of the principal estimate. A tendency is to seize upon that view closest to your own and emphasize it even though it may not be the one of the intelligence community.

3. It seems clear from an examination of the documents published in the several editions of the Pentagon Papers on Vietnam that, if anything, the system was inundated with paper—far beyond the capacity of any senior official to absorb. As a consequence, intelligence estimates became just another opinion, and not a respected one at the highest level of government. It is significant that President Johnson omitted reference to any intelligence analyses in his memoir *The Vantage Point*.[41]

4. Undoubtedly contributing to lessened impact of the intelligence viewpoint on the policy level was evidence of differing interpretations of the available information within the intelligence community, as noted above, and in some instances obvious self-pleading.

The problem of differing views and special pleading was not new or unique to the Vietnam issue. Theodore Sorensen says in his book *Kennedy*:

When Kennedy and McNamara took office, their first review of the National Intelligence Estimates revealed not one but several estimates—and these were likely to coincide in the case of the military intelligence representatives with the strategic views and role of their respective service. The Air

---

[41] An omission pointed out by Chester L. Cooper in "The CIA and Decision Making," *Foreign Affairs*, L, 2 (January 1972), 227.

Force estimate, for example, of Soviet missiles then in being was far higher than that of the Navy.[42]

To balance this adverse criticism there is the evaluation of the estimates by Daniel Ellsberg:

> The persistent, realistic skepticism about long-term non-Communist prospects and about the proposals for improving them—particularly about measures to coerce North Vietnamese leadership—that runs through the twenty-year sequence of these estimates/NIE's on the situation in Southeast Asia is one of the most striking phenomena of the documentation in the Pentagon Papers. The contributions of the Intelligence and Research Branch (INR) of State seem to have been particularly creditable.[43]

On Vietnam there was little or no effort to force a resolution of differences by locking policy-makers and intelligence analysts in a room and forcing them to argue out their differences and reach an agreement. This was done in the Cuban missile crisis and has been done since by the Verification Panel of the NSC used during the SALT negotiations.

5. Not all of the problems are with the intelligence community. There are many at the policy level. Among the officials at the top level of any administration the degree of exposure to intelligence and understanding of what role it can play in policy formulation varies widely. Those who have had military or diplomatic experience or have served in Congress generally are more aware of the strengths and weaknesses of intelligence than those who have had no prior governmental service. The former may be influenced by previous experience and the latter by the fiction and misinformation about intelligence to

---

[42] P. 612.

[43] Daniel Ellsberg, "The Quagmire Myth and the Stalemate Machine," in *Papers on the War* (New York: Simon & Schuster, 1972), n. 73.

which they have been exposed. In either instance the approach is neither scientific nor necessarily useful—nor particularly intelligent.

A random sampling of comments suffices to illustrate. One cabinet member whose department was heavily dependent on intelligence support said after a year in Washington that he really did not know what the CIA did. A retired member of the Joint Chiefs of Staff claimed he had never been briefed on the CIA. One senior officer said he had once been misinformed by intelligence, and therefore would never again pay any attention to it.

There are those at the policy level who consider themselves experts on given areas and subjects and regard intelligence estimates as superfluous and unworthy of attention. There are also those who favor a particular policy and who are unmoved by intelligence analyses which indicate such a policy unwise. And there are those who wait for a consensus to develop and then get on the bandwagon.

In the last analysis, the role played by the intelligence community in the formulation of policy will be established by the President. As the chief executive officer he not only decides on the policy but sets the style. If the President reads the daily intelligence reports each morning, then his principal subordinates will read them—but earlier. If the President reads National Intelligence Estimates, so will the rest. And if the President insists on an intelligence analysis of reaction to U.S. policy, that will become a standard procedure.

One cannot say with certainty that if the policy-makers carefully consider intelligence estimates they will then make the right decision. But it is safe to suggest that intelligence can be an important ingredient in determining policies.

4

Overseas Operations

No intelligence service or system advertises its activity—either foreign or domestic—least of all where it conducts operations on the sovereign territory of another nation. Yet throughout the history of the nation-state, intelligence organizations have attempted to obtain secrets, influence political developments, or conduct insurgency on foreign soil.

In effect, an intelligence service is the invisible arm of a nation's foreign relations charged with activities that cannot be undertaken "officially" or openly. While the principal overseas activity of intelligence services is the collection of information, most are required to engage in many "related to intelligence"—as the U.S. law phrases it—operations ranging from political manipulation to unconventional warfare. A nation's intelligence operations against another come to light in military defeat, when an operation fails, when a knowledgeable officer defects, or when for calculated political reasons the cover is lifted on an intelligence operation.

Following the defeat of Germany in the Second World War, the files of the various German intelligence services not only revealed the extent of Nazi espionage but also were informative of Russian intelligence directed against Germany. Since the Second World War, defections from the Russian intelligence service have exposed vast networks: twelve nets operating in the U.S. government during the war; 115 agents expelled from Great Britain at one time; many others described in the memoirs of former Soviet personnel such as Deriabin, Krivitsky, Petrov, Orlov, Kaznacheev, and scores of others. The United States revealed the extent of its aerial surveillance of Cuba at the time of the 1962 missile crisis by producing U-2 photographs to convince a skeptical world that missile sites were being built in Cuba.

The United States has not been without its defectors, dissidents, and revelations. Each has lifted the cover on some intelligence operations. Some of the disclosures have benefited hostile intelligence services, although many of the revelations by dissidents have been inaccurate and misleading, most such individuals claiming more knowledge than they possess, being interested in headlines and personal profit rather than accuracy.

In many respects, the disclosures have been educational to the American people, who have been immersed in spy fiction for years. The most detailed exposure of U.S. overseas intelligence operations was made in the Pentagon Papers. A selection of directives from that collection is illuminating.

On May 8, 1961, an interdepartmental task force composed of representatives of State, Defense, CIA, ICA (International Cooperation Administration), USIA, and the White House staff forwarded to President Kennedy a study on "A Program of Action for South Vietnam." [1] In this proposal was a sizable package of intelligence operations:

2. MILITARY:
   a. The following military actions were approved by the President at the NSC meeting of 29 April 1961:

. . .

---

[1] Gravel, *The Pentagon Papers*, II, p. 638 (for text).

(4) Install as a matter of priority a radar surveillance capability which will enable the G.V.N. to obtain warning of Communist overflights being conducted for intelligence or clandestine air supply purposes. Initially, this capability should be provided from U.S. mobile radar capability.

(5) Provide MAP [Military Assistance Program] support for the Vietnamese Junk Force as a means of preventing Viet Cong clandestine supply and infiltration into South Vietnam by water. . . .

. . .

(b) The following additional actions are considered necessary to assist the G.V.N. in meeting the increased security threat resulting from the new situation across the Laos–G.V.N. frontier:

(1) Assist the G.V.N. armed forces to increase their border patrol and insurgency suppression capabilities by establishing an effective border intelligence and patrol system, by instituting regular aerial surveillance over the entire area. . . . A special staff element will help the G.V.N. gain the support of nomadic tribes and other border inhabitants, . . .

. . .

5. PSYCHOLOGICAL:

. . .

b. The U.S. Country Team, in coordination with the G.V.N. Ministry of Defense, should compile and declassify for use of media representatives in South Vietnam and throughout the world, documented facts concerning Communist infiltration and terrorists' activities and the measures being taken by the G.V.N. to counter such attacks.

c. In coordination with CIA and the appropriate G.V.N. Ministry, USIS [United States Information Service] will increase the flow of information about unfavorable conditions in North Vietnam to media representatives.

. . .

6. COVERT ACTIONS:

a. Expand present operations in the field of intelligence, unconventional warfare, and political-psychological activities to support the U.S. objective as stated.

b. Initiate the communications intelligence actions, CIA and ASA [Army Security Agency] personnel increases, and funding which were approved by the President at the NSC meeting of 29 April 1961.

c. Expand the communications intelligence actions by inclusion of 15 additional Army Security Agency personnel to train the Vietnamese Army in tactical COMINT operations. . . .

. . .

ANNEX 6

Covert Actions

a. *Intelligence:* Expand current positive and counterintelligence operations against Communist forces in South Vietnam and against North Vietnam. These include penetration of the Vietnamese Communist mechanism, dispatch of agents to North Vietnam and strengthening Vietnamese internal security services. Authorization should be given, subject to existing procedures, for the use in North Vietnam operations of civilian air crews of American and other nationality, as appropriate, in addition to Vietnamese. Consideration should be given for overflights of North Vietnam for photographic intelligence coverage, using American or Chinese Nationalists crews and equipment as necessary.

b. *Communications Intelligence:* Expand the current program of interception and direction-finding covering Vietnamese Communist communications activities in South Vietnam, as well as North Vietnam targets. Obtain further USIB authority to conduct these operations on a fully joint basis, permitting the graphic analysis of American agencies with the Vietnamese to the extent needed to launch rapid attacks on Vietnamese Communist communications and command installations.

This program should be supplemented by a program, duly coordinated, of training additional Vietnamese Army units in intercept and direction-finding by the U.S. Army Security Agency. Also, U.S. Army Security· Agency teams could be sent to Vietnam for direct operations, coordinated in the same manner—Approved by the President at the NSC meeting of 29 April 1961.

c. *Unconventional Warfare:* Expand present operations of the First Observation Battalion in guerrilla areas of South Vietnam, under joint MAAG–CIA sponsorship and direction. This should be in full operational collaboration with the

Vietnamese, using Vietnamese civilians recruited with CIA aid.

In Laos, infiltrate teams under light civilian cover to Southeast Laos to locate and attack Vietnamese Communist bases and lines of communications. These teams should be supported by assault units of 100 to 150 Vietnamese for use on targets beyond capability of teams. Training of teams could be a combined operation by CIA and U.S. Army Special Forces.

In North Vietnam, using the foundation established by intelligence operations, form networks of resistance, covert bases and teams for sabotage and light harassment. A capability should be created by MAAG in the South Vietnamese Army to conduct Ranger raids and similar military actions in North Vietnam as might prove necessary or appropriate. Such actions should try to avoid any outbreak of extensive resistance or insurrection which could not be supported to the extent necessary to stave off repression.

Conduct overflights for dropping of leaflets to harass the Communists and to maintain morale of North Vietnamese population, and increase gray broadcasts to North Vietnam for the same purposes.

d. *Internal South Vietnam:* Effect operations to penetrate political forces, government, armed services and opposition elements to measure support of government, provide warning of any coup plans and identify individuals with potentiality of providing leadership in event of disappearance of President Diem.

Build up an increase in the population's participation in and loyalty to free government in Vietnam, through improved communication between the government and the people, and by strengthening independent or quasi-independent organizations of political, syndical or professional character. Support covertly the GVN in allied and neutral countries, with special emphasis on bringing out GVN accomplishments, to counteract tendencies toward a "political solution" while the Communists are attacking GVN. Effect, in support, a psychological program in Vietnam and elsewhere exploiting Communist brutality and aggression in North Vietnam.

e. *The expanded program* outlined above was estimated to

require an additional 40 personnel for the CIA station and an increase in the CIA outlay for Vietnam of approximately $1.5 million for FY 62, partly compensated by the withdrawal of personnel from other areas. The U.S. Army Security Agency actions to supplement communications intelligence will require 78 personnel and approximately $1.2 million in equipment. The personnel and fund augmentations in this paragraph were approved by the President at the NSC meeting of 29 April 1961.

f. In order adequately to train the Vietnamese Army in tactical COMINT operations, the Army Security Agency estimates that an additional 15 personnel are required. This action has been approved by the U.S. Intelligence Board.[2]

This one directive covers the spectrum of intelligence and counterinsurgency operations from the elementary to the sophisticated, and authorized operations which were to be used for many years to come—with varying organizations and command lines.

For the collection of intelligence, agents were to be sent to North Vietnam, teams to Southeast Laos, and in South Vietnam itself information was sought from within the government, the armed forces, and the opposition in order to gauge the support of the regime, provide warning of coup plans, and discover potential leaders. Both aerial surveillance and photographic overflights were directed and the use of civilian air crews was authorized.[3] Communications intelligence was to provide

[2] There are many other directives and reports on covert operations and intelligence activities in the Pentagon Papers, but none so comprehensive as the above. However, those who would pursue it are referred especially to the Gravel edition, I., Doc. 95, "Lansdale Team's Report on Covert Saigon Mission in 1954 and 1955," p. 95; II, "4. The Overthrow of Ngo Dinh Diem, May–November 1963," pp. 201–76, and "OCO to CORDS," pp. 609–23; III, "Efforts to Improve Intelligence on Progress of the War," pp. 32–34, "Initiation of Covert Operations," pp. 149–54, Doc. 185 "Plan 34 A—September Schedule," p. 553.

[3] Over the years reports have circulated in Southeast Asia about an organization known as Air America, which was written up extensively in an

information through interception of enemy messages, direction-finding to locate hostile transmitters both outside and within South Vietnam, traffic analysis (the volume of traffic is an important clue to the activity of a unit or headquarters), and cryptographic analysis.

Countermeasures, including counterespionage and counterintelligence, were stressed. Radar surveillance was to be developed to watch for clandestine overflights of hostile aircraft to parachute in agents. (This measure seems redundant in Vietnam, where infiltration from the North was never controlled to more than a limited degree.) Junks were to be used to counter maritime infiltration. A system was to be established to patrol the border and collect intelligence. The Communist apparatus in the South was to be penetrated.

In the area of unconventional warfare, political and psychological / operations were authorized to develop support for the South Vietnamese and to attack North Vietnam. Networks and covert bases were to be established in the North to encourage resistance to the Hanoi government and to engage in sabotage. Leaflets were to be dropped over the North (this was four years before the start of the aerial war). "Gray broadcasts" were authorized.[4]

The 1961 operations authorized by President Kennedy on May 11 were followed by others extending the counterinsurgency efforts. On October 13, 1961, authority was given to initiate ground action in Laos against

---

The New York Times entitled "Air America's Civilian Façade Gives It Latitude in East Asia," April 5, 1970. According to that article, this company accepts contracts from AID to provide supplies for Gen. Vang Pao on the Plaine de Jarres in Laos, the Montagnards in Vietnam, etc.

[4] In the war of the air waves, a "gray broadcast" is designed to be of indefinite origin: neither friend nor foe. A "black broadcast," however, is one which you would have the enemy listeners believe originated with their own government.

Communist areial resupply missions in the vicinity of Tchepone, using U.S. advisers, if necessary.[5] Volunteers from the South Vietnamese Army were trained for guerrilla warfare at Nhatrang by a combined staff of forty-five Defense and fifteen CIA officers.[6] The CIA financed the expansion of the South Vietnamese Special Forces for covert war operations, but the support had to be suspended when the Diem regime used these troops against the Buddhists. Harassment operations (known as the 34 A program) against North Vietnam were directed by the Studies and Observation Group of MACV.[7] The Joint Chiefs of Staff said it would be idle to conclude that covert actions would have a decisive effect,[8] while the intelligence community believed there was little chance that " 'progressively escalating pressure' from the clandestine attacks might eventually force Hanoi to order the Vietcong guerrillas in Vietnam and the Pathet Lao in Laos to halt their insurrections." [9]

By the mid-sixties, the counterinsurgency focus shifted from the North to the South and a series of programs was instituted in an effort to accomplish pacification or Vietnamization, or, put more simply, the eradication of the communists from South Vietnam. In 1966 it was called "revolutionary development." Training centers turned out fifty-nine-man teams to put into the villages to battle the VC on the local level. A later operation designed to eliminate the VC infrastructure by capture, defection, or assassination was "PHOENIX." The success can be judged from the evaluation made in NSSM-1 in January 1969. The office of the Secretary of Defense and

[5] *The New York Times, The Pentagon Papers*, p. 88.
[6] *Ibid.*, p. 97.
[7] *Ibid.*, p. 247.
[8] *Ibid.*, p. 248.
[9] *Ibid.*, p. 245.

the CIA believed that: "At present it appears that at least 50 percent of the total rural population is subject to significant VC presence and influence. . . . State (INR) goes even further, saying: 'Our best estimate is that the VC have a significant effect on at least two-thirds of the rural population.' " [10] NSSM-1 adds that one view held that pacification could be achieved in 8.3 years, while another put 13.4 years as the time required.[11]

The organization of the intelligence agencies in Vietnam changed frequently. A CIA mission operated out of the embassy under the direct control of the ambassador. Those CIA personnel engaged in the civic action program reported to a deputy ambassador, together with those from AID and USIA engaged in the same work. There were intelligence personnel at the province and district levels engaged in both civic action and intelligence collection. All of these could be described as the civilian intelligence agencies.

During the period when U.S. forces were engaged in combat, military intelligence personnel were active at all levels. In the field, at the platoon and squad level, the almost constant preoccupation—when not in actual combat with the enemy—was intelligence: patrols into suspected areas (not a popular occupation with the GI's); interrogation of civilians; the constant search for an enemy who seldom wore a uniform and blended with the populace. One need only note that there was intelligence compilation and collection at every level from the squad up the chain of command to MACV: company, battalion, brigade, line divisions, I and II Field Forces, and U.S. Army Vietnam. It should be added that a considerable portion of the final product, together with intelligence

[10] NSSM-1, E 4979.
[11] *Ibid.*, E 4980.

reports from CIA, the embassy, and other U.S. agencies, then went to CINCPAC in Hawaii and to Washington.

One indicator of the extent of U.S. collection activities is given in the National Security Study Memorandum previously cited.[12] It described the sources in Vietnam as follows:

a. Voluminous reports from American advisors, civilian and military, working through Vietnam. These reports are both formal and informal. Some are written, many are conveyed to the Embassy through personal conversations with Embassy officers.

b. Regular contacts by political officers and provincial reporters who operate out of the Embassy. . . .

c. Some limited and relatively unscientific opinion sampling carried out by Vietnamese teams trained and directed by American political officers.

d. Contacts between Embassy officers and foreign journalists, visitors and scholars. Embassy officers seek to tape the knowledge gathered by journalists, scholars and visitors in both written and oral forms.

e. Systematic screening of local publications, including such documents as political party organs as well as editorials in the regular vernacular press.

f. Voluminous reports on the opinions of all these groups gathered through covert contacts by CIA officers and agents.

Vietnam represents the largest intelligence effort by the U.S. government in any one area since the Second World War. In the rest of the world there is no norm for the intelligence effort in any given country. The only criterion that can be given is that the activity of the intelligence agencies will be in direct proportion to the strategic interests of the United States: the more important the area is to American security, the greater the intelligence interest.

[12] *Ibid.*, E 5020.

For example, the United States is committed to the North Atlantic Treaty Organization (NATO). U.S. intelligence is responsible for keeping the government advised of all threats to the NATO area, present and potential. The intelligence effort in Western Europe is large and is centered on the military commands: Supreme Headquarters, Allied Powers Europe in Brussels (SHAPE), Commander-in-Chief Europe in Germany, and its component commands, such as U.S. Army, Europe (USAREUR), U.S. Air Forces, Europe (USAFE) in Ramstein, Germany, and all of the subordinate commands of NATO and the United States. The military intelligence personnel in Europe number in the hundreds.

Throughout Europe, the U.S. embassies also serve as a major source of information through liaison with the host governments: by the ambassador and Foreign Service personnel; by military attachés; by CIA personnel; by legal attachés (FBI personnel assigned overseas for liaison on investigative and security matters); by Treasury Department representatives on economic intelligence and other matters; and by many others, depending on the size of the embassy.

Espionage, or clandestine intelligence collection against the host government in allied or friendly nations, rarely takes place. The basic reason is not so much policy as pragmatism: it is not worth it. If caught, the results can range from embarrassment, through a strain on friendship, to a severance of relations. The Pentagon Papers commented that the CIA ". . . had and has no mandate or mission to perform systematic intelligence or espionage in friendly countries." [13]

Intelligence collection activities against hostile or potentially hostile nations usually take place from third

---

[13] Gravel, *The Pentagon Papers*, II, p. 280.

countries, with or without the consent of the latter. Again, the reasons are practical. Those nations avowedly hostile to the United States have effective police and internal security organizations, as much to keep their own population under control as to thwart foreign espionage. As a consequence, the basic requirement in clandestine collection—picking up information from the agent—becomes dangerous. This is true whether the reports are microfilmed by the agent and put in a hollow log to be picked up later or handed over to another person in a rolled-up newspaper. Consequently, such pickups are best made as far as possible from the local security service.

An understanding of the basic intelligence process is necessary to comprehend these overseas operations. In simplest terms, active collection should be directed only toward that information that cannot be obtained through overt or technical means (photographic or communications).

The first step in the process is to determine precisely what is needed. This is not an easy matter because frequently the policy-maker may not be certain what he wants. "Just give me everything you get" is a too frequent attitude. The most likely requirement is: What will the other nation do? (See the discussion of the Cuban missile crisis in Chapter 3.) The other intelligence consumers at the working level can be much more precise: How deep can a submarine dive? What is the range of a new radar? Does a missile have multiple independently targeted warheads? Once the precise information required is determined, the next question that must be answered is: Where can the information be obtained; either in what documents, or which expert has the answer to the questions? And finally, and most difficult: Who can get to the documents or the person with the information? And how can that individual be recruited?

It may take only a few sentences to describe the process, but it may take months or years to find and recruit the agent. It many cases chance plays a role, although it is not by chance that some of the most valuable spies for the United States have been "walk-ins": men who decided for one reason or another to volunteer information.

The logical conclusion to any discussion of spying is to say that only rarely is the career of an espionage agent a long one with a happy ending. As a result, great efforts are made to obtain information from sources other than the human agent.

An example of an overseas operation of a more esoteric nature was the "Berlin Tunnel." This was discovered by the Russians in 1956 when telephone repairmen, searching for a fault in a cable caused by a rainwater leak along the Schonefelder Chausee, one of the main avenues in East Berlin, discovered a virtual communications center under the street and a tunnel leading to West Berlin. In a rare display of frankness—undoubtedly hopeful of useful propaganda—the Russians invited Western newsmen to see what they had found, pointing out that more than 150 telephone circuits had been tapped and that the tunnel led to an obvious listening post 550 yards away in West Berlin. The circuits included an official Russian tele-printer cable and many military lines. What the Russians did not know, and still don't, is how long the Western allies had been recording all traffic on these cables.[14]

The intelligence community does not have to engage in

[14] See Ian Fleming, "The Great Tunnel into the East Zone," in the Washington *Post*, October 2, 1960, p. 2; also, *The New York Times*, April 25, 1956.

espionage to reach the sensitivities of other nations, as was demonstrated in the case of the Army's CAMELOT operation in 1965. This research project, which attracted worldwide attention, was conducted by the Special Operations Research Office of American University in Washington, D.C., as part of a $20 million Defense Department behavioral science program and was an effort to determine if it is possible to measure and project processes that combine to bring about discontent and revolution in sensitive areas of the world. Chile was the first area selected for study, and when sociologists in that country were questioned by project employees, the Army learned quickly that it was, indeed, a "sensitive" area. On July 8, the project was canceled. On August 2 President Johnson directed the Secretary of State to review all government-sponsored research on foreign areas and people and ordered that "no government sponsorship of foreign area research should be undertaken which in [the Secretary of State's] judgment would adversely affect United States foreign policy." The Secretary of Defense directed that the Pentagon agencies clear such projects with the Assistant Secretary of Defense for International Security Affairs.

On occasion, U.S. intelligence operations overseas embark into the area known as "covert operations." As the name implies, these are supposed to be concealed, secret, and disguised. Further, in the doctrine of any intelligence service, such activities should be "nonattributable": the operation must be so carefully implemented that no trace will lead back to the originating service or nation. Covert operations are not an invention of the CIA nor are they unique to the United States. Efforts to influence developments in other nations by disavowable means are as old as espionage. In modern times, the United States has acknowledged that it has mounted covert operations against Jacobo Arbenz (in Guatemala, 1954, successful)[15] and against Fidel Castro (in Cuba, 1961, unsuccessful).

Space does not permit a detailed description of the disaster at the Bay of Pigs in April 1961. It has been analyzed both from the policy level and the intelligence perspective,[16] and the studies indicate both organizational and substantive failure.

The only participants to acquit themselves with unblemished distinction were those members of the Cuban brigade who landed at the Bay of Pigs. The U.S. government made several errors which are noted here in the hope that they will not be repeated.

1. The operation was mounted by an autonomous unit within the CIA and the full resources neither of the CIA nor of the intelligence community were used to support it.

2. As a result of the above, and most directly because for "security" reasons the intelligence community was not used to analyze the possibilities for success of the operation, the information used (on conditions in Cuba, dissidence in the militia and armed forces, etc.) was subjective and inadequate.

3. The operation became less and less secret. Cubans in Miami talked about volunteers being taken by planeloads from Opa Locka airfield. The Guatemala training base was publicized. If the operation had been covered at the start, by April 1961 the last of the seven veils was fluttering in the breeze and it was exposed. Only the time and place were still secret.

[15] Sorensen, *Kennedy*, p. 296.
[16] See Schlesinger, *A Thousand Days*; Sorensen, *Kennedy*; Hilsman, *To Move a Nation*; Lyman Kirkpatrick, Jr., *The Real CIA* (New York: Macmillan, 1968); Haynes Johnson, *Bay of Pigs* (New York: Norton, 1964); Charles J. V. Murphy, "Cuba: The Record Set Straight," *Fortune*, September 1961.

4. The policy level never was realistically apprised of the chances of success or failure. The President had great confidence in the men running the operation and Allen Dulles told him it had a greater chance of success than the Guatemala operation. But what nobody seemed to have analyzed for the President was how disavowable it would be after it was over, win or lose. President Kennedy was determined that no U.S. forces would be used, but if the operation obviously was American-sponsored, would it make any difference?

In sum, covert operations such as the Bay of Pigs should be used only as the last step in escalation of action to be followed by the use of overt military forces. If a nation is unwilling to take the last step, then any plan for covert action must be dropped or, at least, abandoned when it starts to lose its secrecy.

All overseas intelligence operations raise the fundamental issues of responsibility and control. Who is ultimately responsible for the operations and who exercises the proper control? In the American system the answer is the very top level of the government—in many instances the President himself; in others, the personal delegate of the Chief Executive. President Eisenhower assumed full responsibility for the U-2 operation after a plane was shot down at Sverdlovsk. President Kennedy took the blame for the Bay of Pigs.

Under the President, responsibility rests with the Director of Central Intelligence in Washington and the ambassador or the military commander in the field. Intelligence operations require highly centralized control—and thus direction from Washington is practical—and tightly disciplined personnel. Despite these principles, there have been occasions when field operatives have acted without authority, when individuals have tried to make policy, and when discipline has broken down. Needless to say, there is no government activity where more prompt and drastic corrective action is necessary.

While delegation of authority to the overseas units has on occasion resulted in the breakdown of control, generally the reins are tightly held in Washington. All intelligence collection activities are so controlled, while in the broader field of covert operations or counterinsurgency the original authorization is given by an NSC committee which then periodically reviews the actual results.

5

Domestic Activities

The intelligence community—that is, those agencies concerned exclusively with information on foreign developments—has limited activity and authority within the United States. Only one member of the United States Intelligence Board, the FBI, is responsible for investigating matters within the country affecting the internal security of the nation, although the other members of USIB are responsible for the protection of their own organizations. Basically, the United States, or more precisely, Washington, serves as the headquarters for all of the intelligence agencies, for the final processing of the information for the use of the policy level of the government, and as the command and support base for overseas operations. In many respects, the headquarters staffs of the intelligence agencies in Washington are similar, varying only in size and method. Thus a broad description covers all of the agencies.

The most valuable single asset available to any intelligence service is a body of trained and experienced personnel. Considerable time and attention are devoted to the selection, recruitment, training, and career development of the staff of the intelligence agencies. The general criteria for consideration are good educational background, impeccable personal characteristics, and strong motivation for a lifetime career in intelligence—the last mentioned being especially true for the Central

Intelligence Agency, Defense Intelligence Agency, National Security Agency, and State's INR. To these general criteria could be added a long list of specialties in which the intelligence community is interested: area experts, linguists, communicators, political scientists, physicists, chemists, engineers, administrators, doctors, mathematicians—to mention only a few.

The security and integrity of personnel in the intelligence community is most important, making initial selection and recruitment a most comprehensive procedure. The applicant is required to file extensive questionnaires giving every detail of his/her personal history: date and place of birth of himself/herself and immediate family, all places of residence, jobs, education, travel, membership in organizations, etc. It is the applicant's understanding that he/she will be thoroughly investigated to insure that there is no question about his/her security and loyalty to the United States. Civil libertarians will argue that such an investigation infringes on an individual's constitutional rights and that such rights cannot be waived. If that philosophy were to prevail, there would be no intelligence community and no security or secrecy in government.[1] It is a happy dream and ideal, but not a practical one in modern times; people who want to work in intelligence must give up some freedoms.

The emphasis on personnel security is a practical one, not some mad bureaucrat's personal foible. The American intelligence agencies all have large numbers of

[1] William J. Donovan, head of the Office of Strategic Services in the Second World War, inspired the creation of a special staff to study the type of individual most likely to be a successful intelligence officer. This pioneering effort produced a remarkable study, *Assessment of Men*, by the U.S. Office of Strategic Services, Psychological Assessment Staff (New York: Rinehart, 1948). Also of interest in that area is *The O.S.S. and I* by a member of that staff, William J. Morgan (New York: Norton, 1957).

employees. Most of these people have access to great volumes of highly classified intelligence reports. Only by attempting to insure the absolute loyalty and security of all persons handling classified material can the United Statès keep sensitive information secret. Obviously, the personnel system breaks down at times: people are hired and given security clearances who should not have been; others who were trustworthy initially decide to reveal classified matters for personal or political reasons; some are indiscreet and talk too much.

There are some additional precautions taken to maintain government security. Guards are stationed at all building entrances to check identification cards and in some buildings to examine briefcases and packages. Documents are controlled by recipients being required to sign receipts, but the sheer number of the reports makes this a fragile system. The most sensitive papers may be confined to one room with authorized persons permitted to read them only in the presence of the custodian. However, with tens of thousands of secret reports, only personal security is practical. The closest to absolute security could be insured by searching everybody leaving the buildings, and even this could be frustrated by clandestine means. It is quite true that too many papers are classified, which makes the security problem even more difficult.

The CIA and NSA have specialized staffs engaged in the recruitment and assessment of personnel. The FBI has a careful selection program. In recent years, the military intelligence services have made considerable progress in developing career programs which attract able recruits. The DIA has developed a career service program for their military and civilian personnel. The State Department's Bureau of Intelligence and Research gets its personnel by direct recruitment from Civil

Service rosters and by assignment from the Foreign
Service.

Most training is done in the United States, although
some specialized or technical schooling may take place
overseas in the military commands. The philosophy
behind the training is that intelligence specialists are
made, not born. All intelligence personnel receive some
training whether destined to be analysts, operators, or
support personnel. The subjects range from research
techniques to counterinsurgency, and include courses in
lock-picking, photography, secret writing, and agent
recruitment. If destined for an overseas assignment, an
individual may be given intensive language training at
the Defense Language School, the Foreign Service Institute, or elsewhere. In general, intelligence personnel
receive basic training when entering on duty, further
general schooling in mid-career, and if destined for
executive positions will attend a senior school—possibly
one of the military service war colleges—or get advanced
management training.

Security is important to the intelligence community in
the United States for reasons other than protecting the
thousands of documents. As previously indicated, an
important concern in accepting an applicant for employment is personal security. An individual must be able and
willing to keep a secret, not only during employment but
afterward. Employees are required to sign a statement
upon resignation or retirement in which they agree not to
talk or write about intelligence activities without prior
approval by the agency.[2]

Intelligence personnel in Washington are attractive
targets for other intelligence services. The Czechoslovak

[2] Most employers require discretion on the part of employees. It is
interesting to note that the British have tried to keep secret even the name of
the head of their Secret Intelligence Service.

intelligence service tried, unsuccessfully, to persuade a State Department employee of Czechoslovak ancestry to place a miniature radio transmitter in one of the offices in his department. The Russians have tried to recruit CIA employees. It would be a rich plum, indeed, to place an agent in the headquarters cadre of an American intelligence agency.

The CIA investigates its own applicants for employment and also personnel or organizations that may accept classified contracts from the CIA. By law, the CIA has no police or subpoena powers nor does it engage in any internal security activities—other than those affecting its own personnel or operations. The CIA asks applicants to take a polygraph test; the lie detector, while fallible, is considered a valuable aid to investigation when used by experienced operators.

The FBI has the primary and exclusive responsibility within the United States for the investigation of espionage, sabotage, and subversion, although the CIA, the military services, State, Treasury, and the Atomic Energy Commission obviously will become involved if their personnel or operations are concerned. However, the ultimate jurisdiction in cases of suspected subversion rests with the FBI.

There seems to be relatively little controversy over investigation of espionage, sabotage, or subversion by the FBI as long as foreign agents are involved. The American public accepts, in the interest of national security, the necessity for all types of investigation of potential or obvious espionage against the United States, including the use of telephone taps and electronic listening devices in foreign embassies. Such activity within the United States is under the direction and control of the FBI and is focused on those foreign missions that conduct active intelligence operations against the United States.

The issue of internal security operations becomes highly controversial, however, in the area of potential indigenous threats to the security of the government of the United States. The controversy became particularly acute during the Vietnam War and was reflected in such problems as race riots in the cities, antiwar activists, and student unrest on the university campuses. The question was: Which activists, if any, were a danger to the internal security of the nation and who made the decision as to what constituted a threat—the Attorney General of the United States, the Director of the FBI, the Army, the Federal Courts, or state and local authorities?

Public attention was focused on the overt manifestations of what appeared to be extensive government surveillance using telephone taps, paid informants, and undercover agents. An almost Orwellian atmosphere of "Big Brother is watching you" developed. Serious concern was expressed over the possibilities of a developing police state; extensive literature was produced to document this belief. A Committee for Public Justice was formed to examine the activities of the FBI. A group called Friends of the FBI was organized to respond to the criticism. An organization known as Americans for Effective Law Enforcement was set up in 1966 to counter the American Civil Liberties Union. Antiwar activists stole and published FBI files.

Although many books have been written about the FBI, the most specific details about its operations were published after the office in Media, Pennsylvania, was rifled of its files on March 8, 1971, by persons calling themselves "The Citizens' Committee to Investigate the FBI," and purloined documents were sent to various news media. In March 1972, WIN, a publication of an organization called "Peace and Freedom Through Non-Violent Action" published an assortment of the papers, obviously selected to portray the FBI in the worst possible light.

Included in this publication was a memorandum to all investigative personnel in the Philadelphia office listing 312 companies, government agencies, and other organizations which were to be contacted at least once every six months to develop sources and maintain good will. Another memorandum gave the details on how the National Crime Information Center in the Identification Building in Washington—a computerized record center —was to be used. Others dealt with personnel problems such as the qualifications for special agents. Provisions of the Omnibus Crime Control and Safe Streets Act of 1968 for court orders for wiretaps were cited, and a report of the results of one day's wiretap on the Black Panthers was reproduced. A portion of "New Left Notes" and a request for information on sources in colleges and universities in the area were published together with a number of reports on antiwar activities, the "black left," race problems, the KKK, and draft resisters.

The longest single section of the WIN collection was devoted to a Riot Control Information Bulletin describing civil unrest in some nineteen cities. One collection of the stolen documents dealt with the FBI's counterespionage work and indicated careful surveillance of the Soviet embassy and consular office in Washington, something that will come as no surprise to the Russians. These papers also indicated a concern that American citizens visiting the Soviet Union might be approached as potential recruits by the Russian intelligence services; one document stated that employees of defense contractors who intend to visit Communist countries must advise the Office of Industrial Security Contract Administration Services of the Defense Supply Agency. Particular insight into internal security problems was given in a document entitled "Factors to Be Considered in Deciding Whether an Immigrant or Repatriate Might Have Been Recruited" (by a hostile intelligence service). Among fifty-nine questions to be considered are these: Did he defect? Was defection *bona fide?* If he can speak English, how and why did he learn? Might cooperation have been demanded as the price for permission for spouse's departure from Soviet bloc? If he had a good job, what motivated him to come to the United States? Can he account for the period just before departure for United States? Can he move into a field of intelligence interest? [3]

At issue was genuine concern over the constitutional rights of freedom of speech, assembly, person and property, press, and protest. On the one hand were those who believed that all such rights were being abused, ignored, and progressively restricted on specious and untenable grounds—allegedly to protect national security. At the other extreme were some who were convinced that there was a vast organized conspiracy of anarchists and extremists determined to destroy the American way of life. The courts were in the vise of simultaneously protecting individual rights and the national interest. Evidence that not only inadequate but inaccurate information was being presented to the American people by top officials of the government tended to further exacerbate the situation.

Even more disturbing to many Americans than the FBI internal security operations were revelations in the late sixties of extensive surveillance and investigations of American citizens by the Army. The Army—the uniformed personnel—took the brunt of the criticism for this, even though, as they will be the first to stress, it was

[3] Taken from WIN, "The Complete Collection of Political Documents Ripped-Off from the FBI Office in Media, Pa., March 8, 1971." Box 547, Rifton, New York, 12471.

authorized by competent civilian authority. Alerted in 1967 to the possibility that it might be called on to help suppress civil disorders in as many as one hundred cities, the Army authorized extensive surveillance by every major command in the United States of any potential troublemakers with whom the troops might have to cope in restoring order in the cities. It was not until 1970 that the extent of Army surveillance of civilians started to become publicly known when former soldiers talked about their work as intelligence investigators in the United States. In January 1970 the Subcommittee on Constitutional Rights of the Senate Judiciary Committee, under the chairmanship of Sam J. Ervin, Jr., opened an investigation of the Army's activities that was to last two and a half years. The committee discovered that more than 350 separate record centers contained data on civilian political activity, and that one Army headquarters unit in Texas had a total of 190 linear feet of dossiers and file cards dealing with purportedly subversive organizations and individuals.

According to a press report on September 1, 1972, "a series of highly classified memorandums made available to the New York Times . . ."—by then a most familiar, if not expected, source of information on intelligence activities—gave further details on Army surveillance.[4] According to this report, citizens' band radio communications were monitored by the Army Security Agency on several occasions: during the Republican and Democratic conventions in 1968, the October 1967 march on the Pentagon, the April 1968 riots in Washington, and the June 1968 Poor People's March on Washington. In all instances, the monitoring was approved by the Chief of

[4] "More Army Snooping under Johnson Is Revealed," *The New York Times*, September 1, 1972, 24:1.

Staff of the Army and known to the Attorney General of the United States, even though it was a violation of the Federal Communications Act of 1934.

In December 1970 the Secretary of Defense issued a directive to insure that counterintelligence activities were "completely consistent with constitutional rights, all other legal provisions and national security needs." Secretary Laird's directive stated: "One matter of particular concern to me is the one related to" military investigations of civilian political activity. "Actions have been taken to eliminate some past abuses incident to such activities," he went on to say, "but further corrective actions are necessary as a matter of urgent priority."

The Secretary of Defense ordered a review of Defense Department intelligence activities by an Assistant Secretary of Defense, together with the Secretaries of the Army, Navy, and Air Force, and the Director of the DIA. Mr. Laird further directed that all domestic intelligence gathering by the military services be placed under his policy control.[5] The report of Senator Ervin's subcommittee published in August 1972 verified that it was not until 1970 that the Army's domestic intelligence operations were brought under civilian control.

Assurances by the executive branch that the Army had ceased its surveillance of civilians and destroyed its files were considered insufficient by the American Civil Liberties Union, the Central Committee for Conscientious Objectors, and others who alleged they were targets of the Army's activities, and they sought an injunction to prevent further surveillance and to require destruction of all dossiers. On June 26, 1972, the Supreme Court refused to examine the argument that the Army's surveillance of

---

[5] "Laird Acts to Tighten Rule over Military Intelligence," *The New York Times*, December 24, 1970, p. 1.

civilian political activity was unconstitutional on the grounds that it discouraged criticism of the government. The majority opinion held that control of such surveillance must be left to the Congress and the executive branch. The Court said the argument that the Army's surveillance "chilled" controversy did not seem to be supported, inasmuch as these same political activists had filed the legal action.

In fulfillment of its responsibilities for thwarting espionage, sabotage, and subversion against the United States, the FBI's domestic intelligence unit devotes the greater part of its effort against intelligence personnel of the Soviet Union operating out of its embassy in Washington, out of consulates, out of the United Nations, and through "illegal" networks established by agents under deep cover (similar to the one run by Rudolf Abel, apprehended in 1957 in New York and sentenced to thirty years' imprisonment). The intelligence efforts of the other Communist powers are watched. The third area of concentration is the activities of allegedly radical groups —both of the left and the right—who either have announced intentions of overthrowing the government or who are known to be secretly plotting to do so.

The principal source of information is the paid informer, most of whom volunteer themselves to the FBI. The FBI rarely divulges the names or numbers of its informers. The public learns of their existence only when "surfaced" to testify in court. It would be safe to speculate that their numbers are not large and are concentrated in the Communist party and other extremist groups.[6]

[6] According to an Associated Press report of September 12, 1972, published in *The New York Times*, the Ku Klux Klan ordered the polygraph test for all Klansmen. One Klan official was quoted as saying: "The first purpose we have to solve is this informants business. We have to fight the FBI first. Then we can start on other goals."

A second source of information in the internal security field is direct surveillance. Here, too, there is a great deal of misinformation due to the "Big Brother is watching" syndrome. Direct surveillance takes training and skill, especially if the individual to be watched is an experienced intelligence operator or dedicated revolutionary. Even the FBI, one of the most respected criminal investigation agencies in the world, has its limitations, as simple mathematics show.

It takes at least four men to keep one individual under full-time surveillance—two on duty at all times for twelve-hour shifts, watching front and back entrances to a building or following—and may require twice that number if travel is involved or the suspect is trying to shake his "tail." [7] The FBI has an authorized strength of 8,700 special agents, operating from fifty-nine field offices in the United States. Most of the special agents are assigned to criminal matters, and only a relatively small percentage detailed to espionage or subversion. If one takes a figure of about 10 percent for the effort on internal security, which may be high, and assumes that half of those 800 special agents are following leads, working on files, testifying in court, or attending to the multitude of other details inevitable in such work, that leaves 400 for surveillance; and then if one settles on the smallest surveillance squad possible—four—only 100 suspects could be watched at any one time. If one takes the figure of 400 Soviet Union personnel stationed in the United States and uses a figure of 50 percent engaged in intelligence work (the usual estimate is higher, 60 to 70 percent), you conclude that less than half could be watched by the FBI at any one time. This leaves no FBI

[7] For those who would pursue this aspect, there are books and manuals available on surveillance techniques in most public libraries.

personnel for the surveillance of homegrown subversives.

The above example obviously is oversimplified for the sake of illustration, and there are many qualifications. For example, a number of the Russian intelligence personnel are engaged in nothing more sinister than clipping newspapers or reading Government Printing Office publications. Some are just wandering around looking for someone who might know something that would interest Moscow. There are only a few known to be trying to recruit agents or get classified information: for example, a Russian UN employee tried to buy information about the new Navy F-14 fighter plane from a Grumman employee and was arrested in the act. So the number under surveillance can be limited.

In the public mind, wiretapping and the use of electronic surveillance devices by police and security agencies assume vast and ubiquitous proportions. The use of such techniques in the decades following the Second World War in criminal and national security cases became a major constitutional issue before the courts.

A brief review of the legal history of wiretapping is revealing. In 1928 the Supreme Court refused to declare wiretapping unconstitutional. In 1940 President Roosevelt authorized the FBI to use wiretaps in suspected espionage cases. In 1942 the Supreme Court went so far as to uphold the legality of the use of a "detectaphone," a device that could be held against certain types of walls and thereby transmit conversations on the other side of the partition. President Truman in 1946 broadened the authority for wiretaps to include American citizens suspected of espionage.

In 1965 President Johnson ordered the federal government to stop all electronic eavesdropping except for cases involving national security, and in those cases only when authorized in advance by the Attorney General.

In 1967 the Supreme Court ruled that a conversation was protected by the Fourth Amendment to the Constitution. The Court also ruled that a New York State statute authorizing wiretapping in certain cases was unconstitutional because it did not provide for sufficient judicial control.

In 1968 the Congress passed the Omnibus Crime Control Act. This law authorizes state and local police to obtain warrants from a judge to wiretap or eavesdrop in cases involving a commission or potential commission of any crime punishable by more than a year in prison. The warrants, which are also required in national security cases, are good for thirty days but can be renewed for thirty-day periods indefinitely. In case of emergency, a wiretap can be made and a warrant obtained later, but within forty-eight hours. Ninety days after a wiretap is removed the person involved must be notified, although a judge can postpone this. Any individual receiving such a notice can sue the authorizing authority for damages if the subject of the wiretap feels he has been overheard without just cause. The law also banned the interstate shipment of listening devices.

On June 19, 1972, in a unanimous 8 to 0 decision, Justice William H. Rehnquist abstaining, the Supreme Court ruled that warrants were required in cases of domestic subversion, but did not render an opinion on foreign intelligence activities in the United States, saying:

> . . . The instant case requires no judgment on the scope of the President's surveillance power with respect to the activities of foreign powers, within or without this country. The Attorney General's affidavit in this case states that the surveillances were "deemed necessary to protect the nation from attempts of domestic organizations to attack and subvert the existing structure of Government." There is no evidence of any involvement, directly or indirectly, of a foreign power.

Excerpts from the opinion rendered by Justice Lewis F. Powell, Jr., indicate the reasoning of the Court:

> We begin the inquiry by noting that the President of the United States has the fundamental duty, under Article II, Section 1 of the Constitution, "to preserve, protect and defend the Constitution of the United States."
>
> Implicit in that duty is the power to protect our Government against those who would subvert or overthrow it by unlawful means.
>
> In the discharge of this duty, the President—through the Attorney General—may find it necessary to employ electronic surveillance to obtain intelligence information on the plans of those who plot unlawful actions against the Government.
>
> . . .
>
> But those charged with this investigative and prosecutional duty should not be the sole judges of when to utilize constitutionally sensitive means in pursuing their tasks.
>
> . . .
>
> We cannot accept the Government's argument that internal security matters are too subtle and complex for judicial evaluation. Courts regularly deal with the most difficult issues of our society.
>
> If the threat is too subtle or complex for our senior law enforcement officers to convey its significance to a Court, one may question whether there is probable cause for surveillance.
>
> Nor do we believe prior judicial approval will fracture the secrecy essential to official intelligence gathering.
>
> . . .
>
> Although some added burden will be imposed upon the Attorney General, this inconvenience is justified in a free society to protect constitutional values. Nor do we think the Government's domestic surveillance powers will be impaired to any significant degree.
>
> By no means of least importance will be the reassurances of the public generally that indiscriminate wiretapping and bugging of law-abiding citizens cannot occur.[8]

[8] *The New York Times*, June 20, 1972, 1:1.

Two months later, in a case involving the release of the Pentagon Papers, the Justice Department, in a petition to the Supreme Court, approved search warrants in those cases involving "foreign intelligence." Thus the issue of what constituted a threat to national security was still very much in contention.

The extent of this type of surveillance was given in a report prepared by Professor Herman Schwartz of the State University of New York at Buffalo for the American Civil Liberties Union. The report, entitled "Summary of the Findings on the Amount, Benefits and Costs of Official Electronic Surveillance," indicated that in 1970 there were 597 court orders, federal, and state authorized wiretaps in which 381,865 conversations were overheard, involving 25,652 persons. To place this in proper context, it is estimated that in 1970 in the United States there were 465 million telephone conversations every twenty-four hours.

Reports on different periods give a perspective on the number of federal electronic surveillance operations. During the Second World War there were as many as 140. At one point in 1965 there were thirty-two. On December 15, 1971, there were thirty-two telephone taps and four microphones in operation. In June 1972, after the Supreme Court ruled that warrants must be obtained in national security cases, the Justice Department reported twenty-seven wiretaps for foreign intelligence. Obviously, the number fluctuates in proportion to the activity of the suspected or exposed hostile intelligence operations.

Like other forms of counterespionage, electronic surveillance is difficult and expensive. The equipment involved is costly and sophisticated and must be manned by trained experts. There are many ways to tap a telephone, not the least important requirement being that the tap be undetected. Placing a "bug" or micro-phone requires even more talent, including surreptitious entry. Once the tap or microphone is in place, either teams of monitors are required to listen to the conversa-tions or recorders are used to tape the calls. If the latter, the tapes will have to be replayed to glean the items of intelligence, if any. If the conversations are in foreign languages, then translators or bilingual monitors are required. Finally, if the suspects are foreign agents, depending on their training and experience, they will avoid saying anything of significance over any telephone which might be tapped or in any room which could be bugged; they will use prearranged codes, or they will use a different pay telephone for each call. There are 1,489,343 public and semipublic telephones in the United States: 90,400 in the New York City area alone and 21,800 in Washington. To tap a public phone without knowing it will be used by a suspect is futile.

How much the intelligence community benefits in the form of valuable information produced through internal security operations is difficult to evaluate. The intensity of intelligence operations mounted against the United States is in itself an important clue to foreign policy objectives of the other government. The types of informa-tion that agents are directed to obtain and the questions they ask are informative. Most valuable of all is when a foreign agent can be persuaded to defect and tell all.

In many respects the federal government is a very junior partner in the field of investigative work within the United States, and within the federal arena the activities of the intelligence community are small by comparison. Exclusive of the intelligence system, a brief sampling of departments and agencies engaged in some domestic investigation would include the Internal Revenue Serv-ice, Federal Communications Commission, Postal Inspection Service, Food and Drug Administration, Federal Bureau of Narcotics and Dangerous Drugs, Federal Trade Commission, Securities and Exchange Commission, Civil Aeronautics Board, Alcohol and Tobacco Tax Division, Immigration and Naturalization Service, Civil Service Commission, Fish and Wildlife Service, and the Coast Guard.

At the state and local level, the numbers increase geometrically. Most large modern police departments now include an Intelligence Division, a unit that does exactly what its name implies: tries to find out about crimes before they happen. If the Army is concerned about civil unrest in the cities, the state and local police are even more so: they are in the front lines domestically, and the National Guard and federal units are the reserves behind them. For many years there have been "red" units in some police departments to follow the activities of local Communists. In recent years, where the situation warranted, these units have become responsible for coverage of all extremist and potential subversive or revolutionary groups. Most such work is carried on in close collaboration with the FBI and federal authorities.

On February 9, 1973, New York City Police Commissioner Patrick V. Murphy announced that index cards on 980,000 persons and 100,000 organizations had been purged from the Intelligence Division files on public security matters, reducing the number of index cards of persons in the files to 240,000 and of organizations to 25,000. The number of intelligence folders on individuals was reduced from 3,500 to 2,500 and on organizations from 1,500 to 200. The commissioner also announced that the department had developed written guidelines to control the gathering, processing, and dissemination of intelligence information. Guidelines cited indicated that intelligence investigations on all matters outside of organized crime or infiltration of a suspected organization could be undertaken only with specific approval of a senior officer; political beliefs alone could not be justification for an investigation; dissemination of intelligence information to other governmental agencies could be authorized only by the commander of the Intelligence Division in response to written requests.[9]

Of course, the New York City files should not be viewed as typical, amounting to nearly one name for every eight persons in the city until the purging. Commissioner Murphy noted that the files had become dated and that many names were no longer of interest. Further, many police departments in smaller cities and towns do not have intelligence divisions. However, assuming that the remaining names, 240,000, represent true "intelligence" interest, it would be a proportion of one out of every thirty-three persons. Projecting this to the thirty-three largest metropolitan areas with a 1970 population of 80,684,000 people, and assuming those areas had centralized intelligence files, which they do not, it is conceivable that 2,748,000 names could be on file.

In sum, how many investigative agencies are directly concerned with the security and loyalty of the American citizen? The federal agencies involved are the FBI, the Defense Investigation Service (created in 1972 as a centralized service to investigate personnel for the Defense Department and presumably to eventually take over all such matters from the Army, Navy, and Air Force), and the Civil Service Commission. As noted, the CIA would be involved only in investigating its own applicants for employment and the persons and organizations with which it has business. Add to these state and local police forces and investigative agencies.

[9] *The New York Times*, February 9, 1973.

How many people are investigated? The number must run well over a million a year. These would include all persons either applying for employment in the federal government or in industry where there would be access to classified matters. If one takes a standard annual turnover of personnel of about 30 percent and uses as a base 3,449,366 federal civilian employees in State and Defense, and military personnel, this would require 1,034,808 investigations of new people each year. Over a twenty-year period there could be an accumulation of some 20,696,160 files.

If one adds to this such categories as travelers to Communist countries and immigrants or repatriates who are potential recruits for hostile intelligence services, radicals of the left or right, student activists, antiwar groups, and draft resisters, and accords to these groups perhaps an overly generous proportion of one-half of one percent of the population, another 1,100,000 names would be added.

The magnitude of domestic security investigations can be appreciated if one assumes that a minimum of twenty persons are contacted in each case, which would give a total of more than twenty million interviews each year.

Some of the agencies in the intelligence community use domestically based facilities to support overseas operations. The history of intelligence operations is replete with descriptions of devices used to facilitate not only clandestine collection but "intelligence-related" projects in the broad fields of political action and irregular warfare. Without such facilities—cover organizations, funding mechanisms, transportation companies—the intelligence agencies would be unable to carry out their responsibilities, and the U.S. government would be deprived of an instrument of foreign policy. Whether the mere availability of such an instrumentality leads policy-makers to make use of covert operations which reflect adversely on American integrity will be discussed further.

While there were many reports and rumors of organizations in the United States that provided cover for intelligence, it was not until the mid-sixties that a series of articles described them. The April 1966 issue of *Ramparts* magazine reported that a program for the training of police officers in South Vietnam conducted by the Police Administration School of Michigan State University had given cover and support to the CIA from 1955 to 1959. The facts that emerged from this eye-catching exposure—glamorized by a flashy cover drawing portraying Madame Nhu as a cheerleader wearing an MSU sweater—were these. Michigan State University, an institution with an international reputation for its police school and graduate work in criminology, received a contract from AID to assist in the training of Vietnamese police. Five men were borrowed from the government to assist. These were CIA employees, all former police officers and specialists in countersubversion.

The revelations immediately brought an inquiry by the legislature of the State of Michigan. The concerned university pointed out that the CIA men had been transferred to another part of the U.S. mission in Saigon in 1959 and that it had halted counterinsurgency training. A shadow was cast on other Michigan State-sponsored projects, such as the National Institute of Community Development in Hyderabad, India, an AID project to develop techniques to accelerate change in agriculture. S. C. Gupta of the Agriculture Economic Research Center at Delhi University was quoted as saying, "The United States has been using university research projects as a cover for the Central Intelligence Agency to subvert governments in several countries." [10] Other American

[10] *The New York Times*, May 7, 1966.

endeavors in India also were under suspicion. A proposal by President Johnson for an Indian-American Foundation was attacked by AGE, the official organ of the right-wing Communist party of India, in an article entitled "Beware of the CIA," as an effort to "further expand the field of the CIA operation in India." H. J. Mukerjee, the parliamentary leader of the right-wing Communists, submitted a resolution to oppose the foundation as "another of those gold-plated grinding stones which we are importing from America to wear around our necks." [11]

In April 1966 *The New York Times* published a series of five lengthy articles about the CIA reviewing both the known and the unknown and examining such questions as: Was it out of control of its supposed political masters? Was it damaging the national interest while it sought to advance it? Did it lie to influence political leaders so that it was an "invisible government"? Was it becoming a burden on American foreign policy? The *Times* articles, written by some of its top reporters and based on months of inquiries and research, reviewed known CIA successes and failures and false allegations against it and described in detail its organization.[12] The *Times*, while critical of some CIA actions, did not find the expected ogre and gave the agency a creditable report.

In March 1966 Congressman Wright Patman, Chairman of the House Select Committee on Small Business, in the course of an examination of tax-exempt foundations by Subcommittee No. 1 on Foundations, revealed that the J. M. Kaplan Fund had been operating as a conduit for channeling CIA funds, and named several other foundations that he characterized as CIA fronts.[13]

[11] *Ibid.*
[12] *The New York Times*, April 25–29, 1966.
[13] *The New York Times*, March 5, 1966.

In February 1967 a former employee of the National Student Association revealed that for some years that organization had been subsidized by the CIA and claimed that students were used to gather intelligence. It emerged that CIA support to the NSA had started in 1950 with a grant of $12,000 to send a team to Europe and Africa to study student groups. Over the years the CIA subsidy to the NSA increased until it amounted to 80 percent of the income of the student organization, used primarily in the international affairs program to send American student delegations abroad to youth meetings to provide a free-world voice and to give financial assistance to non-Communist left-wing student organizations. Only the top two officers in the NSA had been aware that the CIA had been the original source of the funds.

The NSA report was followed by a series of news stories identifying other CIA-supported organizations: the Congress for Cultural Freedom, the Cooperative League of the U.S.A., the American Newspaper Guild, the World Confederation of Organizations of the Teaching Profession, the Asia Foundation, and the American Friends of the Middle East. There was immediate worldwide reaction. President Johnson named a three-man committee chaired by Under Secretary of State Nicholas Katzenbach to look into the matter and report to him.

The academic world was particularly concerned about the effects. Robert A. Dahl, president of the American Political Science Association, named a committee to investigate CIA penetration of the academic community and was quoted as saying, "There are bound to be evil effects." The president of the Berkeley student body said, "The credibility of U.S. students abroad is greatly damaged." [14] Twenty-two faculty members of Vassar College urged the students to beware of the CIA's recruiting efforts on the campus.[15] In Madrid, the Falangist newspaper *Arriba* quoted *Ramparts* as saying that an NSA agent had conspired with antiregime students: according to *The New York Times*, the NSA representative for Spain and Latin America had taken part in a three-day sit-in at a Capuchin monastery in Barcelona in March 1966 and had been arrested and expelled from Spain.[16] The American Anthropological Association, by a 729 to 59 vote of its 4,400 members, adopted this resolution:

> Academic institutions and individual members of the academic community, including students, should scrupulously avoid both involvement in clandestine intelligence activities and the use of the name anthropology, or the title of anthropologist as a cover for intelligence activities." [17]

The American political reaction was varied and did not follow party lines. Vice President Hubert Humphrey was quoted as saying he was "not at all happy about what CIA had been doing. . . . Out of this, I hope will come an agreement to keep CIA out of student affairs." Senator Robert Kennedy said, "If the policy was wrong, it was not the product of CIA, but of each administration." Senator Richard Russell: "All of this clamor about impairing academic freedom or subverting youth is a lot of hogwash!" [18] Senator Everett Dirksen said it was "little more than a Roman holiday." [19] On the television pro-

---

[14] *Time* (March 3, 1967), p. 23.
[15] *The New York Times*, February 24, 1967.
[16] *Ibid.*
[17] Providence *Journal*, April 8, 1967.
[18] *Time* (March 3, 1967), p. 23
[19] *The New York Times*, February 25, 1967.

gram "Face the Nation," Senator Barry Goldwater argued: "Why didn't they spread it around? In other words, what they have been doing with it as far as I can see, is to finance Socialism in America." [20]

Joseph Kraft, a Washington-based columnist wrote: "Intrinsically the agency's practice of giving secret support to groups of students and other persons is a trivial affair. It did not debase free institutions nor baffle unfree ones. . . . But symbolically . . . it is the problem of how we run the country." [21]

Another view was taken by James P. Brown, editorial writer for the Providence *Journal*, in an article entitled "One Man's Opinion: A Broad Pattern of Deceit Threatens U.S. Freedoms":

> It is disturbing that there are still many Americans who do not yet recognize the risk we run in attempting to beat an enemy at his own despicable game.
>
> The crisis provoked by the current revelations has been greatly compounded by the fact that it has landed in the middle of a widening credibility gap. . . . We are forced to recognize that deceit has become an accepted instrument of national policy.
>
> . . . It is now becoming apparent that where we have imitated Communist tactics, we have done ourselves more harm than good.
>
> . . . candor and fundamental honesty—a traditional American characteristic that has carried far more weight abroad than most Americans realize.[22]

Washington officials were quoted as fearing that the disclosures would hurt the work of the CIA. Laszlo Szabo, a former major in the Hungarian Intelligence

---

[20] As quoted in *The New York Times*, February 27, 1967, in an article, "Goldwater Says CIA Is Financing Socialism in U.S."

[21] Providence *Journal*, February 27, 1967.

[22] Providence *Journal*, February 27, 1967.

Service, said he was amazed at the "naïve attitude of the Americans about propaganda. It is the front in the secret war." Wladyslaw Tykocinski, former chief of the Polish military mission in West Berlin, echoed the same feeling: "You Americans simply do not understand that the motivation of Communist activity in the west is relentlessly political. They flatter the intellectuals and the non-Communist left and they get them to do the work. They don't want them as Communist party members but as stooges who have entrée in society." [23]

Organizations that had received CIA money rejected any allegations that the agency had influenced their actions. The trustees of the Asia Foundation announced that they had knowingly received money from foundations which had received it from the government, but would no longer do so. They said that foundation personnel "have not been used or influenced in any way, directly or indirectly, by any contributor to the foundation." [24] Harvard University, which received $456,000 from organizations acting as conduits for the CIA, said there had been no conditions.[25] Stanley Dreyer, president of the Cooperative League, said he was not concerned that the money originated with the CIA: "We'd be willing to take money from the devil himself if no strings were attached." [26] *Encounter*, a British-American review, was supported by funds from the Congress for Cultural Freedom, an organization of leading American and European intellectuals, which in turn was financed in large part by the CIA. Melvin Lasky, the editor, made the comment, "In fact, as it turned out, *Encounter*, like many other political, educational and cultural institutions

[23] *The New York Times*, March 6, 1967.
[24] *The New York Times*, March 22, 1967.
[25] Providence *Journal*, April 15, 1967.
[26] *The New York Times*, May 16, 1967.

throughout the world, was an unwitting recipient of funds which derived indirectly from the CIA." He went on to say that *Encounter*'s editorial policy had never been affected: "We were fair, critical, controversial. We have tried to publish articles pro and con on every major intellectual issue—Vietnam, Cuba, everything . . . that anyone tried to manipulate material improperly is ridiculous." [27]

A year after the disclosures, the Washington *Post* did an article reviewing what had happened to three of the organizations formerly subsidized by the CIA and made the comment, "Their beneficiaries in the developing world barely raised an eyebrow over the disclosures." [28]

The committee established by President Johnson to study the CIA subsidies made its initial report on February 22, 1967:

> When the Central Intelligence Agency lent financial support to the work of certain American private organizations, it did not act on its own initiative but in accordance with national policies established by the National Security Council in 1952 through 1954. Throughout, it [the intelligence agency] acted with the approval of senior interdepartmental review committees, including the Secretaries of State and Defense or their representatives. These policies have, therefore, been in effect under four Presidents.[29]

On March 30 the White House released the final report signed by Under Secretary of State Katzenbach, Secretary of Health, Education and Welfare John W. Gardiner, and Director of Central Intelligence Richard M. Helms. It contained two basic recommendations:

> 1. It should be the policy of the United States Government that no Federal Agency shall provide any covert financial

[27] *The New York Times*, May 9, 1967.
[28] Washington *Post*," "Much Different without CIA Aid."
[29] Letter from Under Secretary of State Nicholas Katzenbach to President Johnson.

assistance or support, direct or indirect, to any of the Nation's educational or private voluntary organizations.

2. The Government should promptly develop and establish a public-private mechanism to provide public funds openly for overseas activities of organizations which are adjudged deserving, in the national interest of public support.

In explaining its recommendations the committee said:

The work of private American organizations, in a host of fields, has been of great benefit to scores of countries. That benefit must not be impaired by foreign doubts about the independence of these organizations. The Committee believes it is essential for the United States to underscore that independence immediately and decisively.[30]

The Katzenbach-Gardiner-Helms report was precise in saying that there should be no covert support for any educational, philanthropic, or cultural organizations at any time. President Johnson immediately announced his approval of the report and directed all concerned government agencies to implement. The following week he appointed an eighteen-member committee drawn from government and private areas, headed by Secretary of State Dean Rusk, to recommend methods for providing open assistance to private and voluntary organizations. Thirteen months later, in May 1968, this committee recommended the creation of a public commission to be provided with funds by the Congress to support worthwhile projects but suggested that no action be taken until the new administration took office in January 1969. And there the matter rests.

Two other CIA-subsidized organizations, neither private nor voluntary, Radio Free Europe and Radio

---

[30] The full text of the report, as released, is contained in the Washington *Post*, March 30, 1967.

Liberty, were funded through appropriations to the State Department for fiscal year 1972.

In sum, the activities of the intelligence community within the United States range from recruitment and investigation of staff personnel through investigations of potential threats to internal security to sizable headquarters in Washington. At the height of the Cold War, the CIA used front organizations for political warfare, an activity now banned by Presidential directive. In many respects, the constant scrutiny to which all government activities are subjected by the press serves as a check on secret activities of the United States.

6

Sources of Political Support and Criticism

The intelligence community has little or no political constituency. What support it has among the electorate comes from individuals and small groups supporting one agency or another, not the intelligence community as a whole, and generally without much impact. Usually, the same people and organizations who support a strong military defense posture also favor a major intelligence effort.

The public attitude toward intelligence, as it is toward other government activities that do not have a direct or personal impact, is one of acceptance as long as the agencies appear to be producing the information necessary for national security. On the other hand, when intelligence intrudes into an area where it raises questions about the integrity of an entire segment of society, such as academia, there is a strong public reaction, especially by those directly affected. When the U-2 aircraft was shot down over Russia in 1960, some individuals expressed concern that the intelligence agencies might be engaged in provocative acts that could get the United States into a war. When President Diem of South Vietnam was assassinated in a military coup in November 1963, many in the United States were certain it was a CIA operation. The implied involvement of the CIA in incidents in Guatemala, Iran, Indonesia, and Singapore, to name a few, makes it a prime suspect—not just to

Americans but to much of the world—every time there is a plot, a coup, or violent political change.

The Central Intelligence Agency follows a policy to "neither confirm nor deny" allegations made about it. On only rare occasions does Congress comment, and then not with one voice. Even more rarely does the President feel required to defend the CIA. Thus the silence that follows most incidents leaves the public with questions unanswered and ready to accept the validity of unchallenged allegations.

In a world in the midst of a technological revolution which includes an explosion of information and a vast expansion of the public media, many things that went undetected a few years ago now become widely known. The number of incidents involving some form of clandestine activity somewhere in the world, even though most are not of American origin or interest, serves as a constant reminder of the hidden war of the intelligence services. Those of the American people who pay any attention to such matters are inclined to believe that the CIA is involved. Frequent press speculation about the number of persons employed by the CIA and the size of a budget reputed to run into the hundreds of millions or billions of dollars serves to increase public concern.

A sample of questions asked about the CIA is illustrative.[1]

What is a typical budget for the CIA?
Was the CIA responsible for analyzing the Gulf of Tonkin incident which led to the bombing of North Vietnam, and, if so, why is the Foreign Relations Committee denied access to the reports?

[1] These are from thirty questions submitted in writing to the author during the question-and-answer period following a lecture at Rhode Island Junior College in Providence in 1969. Of the questions asked, four each dealt with the Kennedy assassination, the subsidy to NSA, the Bay of Pigs, and Vietnam.

Did CIA construct a defense plan for the march on the Pentagon?

What were the reasons the CIA was involved in the overthrow of one of our so-called allies—that is the overthrow of the Diem regime in South Vietnam?

Do agents follow H. Rap Brown, Stokely Carmichael, and other pro-Communists?

Is intelligence always evaluating information for military or defense implications?

Would you explain why CIA was so inept in the Bay of Pigs fiasco, while the Russian intelligence service successfully infiltrated Castro's government without the intervention of the CIA?

What security clearance (if any) is held by members of Congress and how is their loyalty determined?

What is your reaction to District Attorney Garrison's accusations about the CIA involvement in the Kennedy assassination?

It has been stated that the CIA has no political affiliation, yet why has it been subsidizing certain groups, the outstanding one being the Student Non-Violent Coordinating Committee?

How involved has the CIA become in the revolutionary movement in South America?

If CIA is primarily a foreign intelligence agency, what is it doing on the campus—subsidizing, etc?

Recently in the newspapers there was an article about well-educated people in Saigon believing that the CIA was behind counteracts such as bombing the U.S. Embassy. Is this true?

Does the CIA influence internal control through mass media, influence on the President, and influence on existing "brother agencies"?

Projection: Is the CIA emerging as a new form of internal government of the United States?

Do you feel the future of CIA will brighten?

These questions are typical and reflect interest, concern, and ignorance about the work of the CIA and the intelligence community.

Publicity about American intelligence activities provides grist for the propaganda mills of the Soviet
Union—as does any commentary about defects in our
system. In the five years from 1965 through 1969, papers
and journals in the Soviet Union printed more than one
hundred articles annually purportedly about Western
intelligence activities, with the U.S. agencies receiving
the bulk of the attention.[2] Of the intelligence agencies,
the CIA was discussed in nearly one-third of all articles
about Western intelligence services. Only a dozen or so
articles discussed the FBI, and about the same number
the intelligence agencies of the Defense Department.
However, all overseas arms of the U.S. government were
assumed by the Soviet authors and editors to be part of
the intelligence system; the State Department, the
United States Information Agency, and the Peace Corps
received particular attention. The cancellation of the
CAMELOT project received headlines in Moscow.[3] The
allegations by New Orleans District Attorney James
Garrison that CIA agents were implicated in the assassination of President Kennedy were the subject of several
articles.[4]

The extensive coverage of Western intelligence activities by the media of the Soviet Union serves a dual
purpose. As propaganda, it is one of the constant
reminders to the Russian people to beware of foreign
intelligence activities. As psychological warfare, it keeps
the activities of the American intelligence services in the
press of the world; many of the articles are repeated by

---

[2] For a listing of some 590 articles gleaned from the press of the Soviet
Union, see "Soviet Intelligence and Security Services, 1964–70: A Selected
Bibliography of Soviet Publications with Some Additional Titles from Other
Sources," prepared by the Congressional Research Service, Library of Con-
gress (Washington: Government Printing Office, 1972).

[3] *Ibid.*, p. 242.

[4] *Ibid.*, pp. 243, 245, 252, 254.

news media in other countries. This serves to create and
enhance fears of U.S. meddling and causes a backlash
even in the United States. Whether it is fact or fiction is
not important. Denials usually are ineffective, and in
most instances the accused intelligence services will
refrain from comment.

A sampling of titles alone is revealing:

"How to Recognize a CIA Agent" (Moscow: *Komsomolskaya Pravda*, April 30, 1966)

"You Will Fulfill All Assignments. Statements of a Former
American Spy" (Vilnyus: *Svyturys* nos. 19, 20, and 21, October 1964)

"The Alliance Between the Neo-Nazis and the CIA"
(Moscow: *Izvestya*, February 14, 1968)

"The Tentacles of CIA" (Moscow: *Moskovskaya Pravda*,
and Riga: *Sovetskaya Latviya*, August 21, 1968; Moscow:
Isvestya, August 2, 1968; Kiev: *Pravda Ukrainy*, May 17,
1967)

Descriptive—and imaginative—articles warn the Third
World of American intelligence:

"The CIA and the Pentagon in Africa" (Riga: *Sovetskaya
Latviya*, March 5, 1968)

"CIA Maneuvers in Peru" (Moscow: *Pravda*, July 14,
1969)

"American Espionage in Northern Europe" (Moscow:
Novoye Vremya, no. 33, August 16, 1968)

"Quiet Americans in Laotian Jungles" (Moscow: *Pravda*,
July 9, 1969)

"CIA Tentacles in the Near East" (Moscow: *Pravda*,
December 6, 1968)

"CIA Rushes to the Apennines" (Moscow: *Nedelya*, June
16, 1968)

The Soviet Press also is adept in spreading further the
impression that the CIA is involved in everything and, of
course, is anxious to discredit the agency whenever
possible, as the following sampling illustrates:

"Who's Who in CIA" (Moscow: *Novoye Vremya*, no. 29, July 19, 1968)

"A University as a Branch of the CIA" (Moscow: *Pravda*, October 3, 1966)

" 'Philanthropists' from the CIA Are Packing Their Suitcases" (Moscow: *Pravda*, May 23, 1968)

"Group 54-12 Issues the Orders" (Moscow: *Nedelya*, October 22–28, 1967)

"An Ambassador in the Service of the CIA" (*Komsomolskaya Pravda*, July 9, 1968)

"Agronomists from the CIA" (Moscow: *Pravda*, May 20, 1967)

"CIA—Impresario of Culture" (Moscow: *Literaturnay Gazeta*, July 30, 1969 [taken from the U.S. *Ramparts* magazine])

"CIA's Supplier Herbert Marcuse" (Moscow: *Trud*, August 2, 1969)

"CIA Against Peasants" (Moscow: *Izvestya*, March 15, 1968)

The Russians even translated and published *The Invisible Government* by Wise and Ross (*Nevidimoye Pravitelstvo*; Moscow: Voyennoye Izdatelstvo Ministersva Oborony SSSR, 1965, 304 pp.).

How much impact this attention to Western intelligence has on the people of the Soviet Union is impossible to judge. It is rarely seen by most Americans, except when reported by the Western press. It may receive some attention in the newer nations.

Perhaps more effective in the constant struggle between the intelligence services is the so-called disinformation program of the Soviet State Security Committee, which keeps the CIA under fairly constant attack. The favorite battleground for attack by the Disinformation Bureau is to float an article or book in the public media of the West and then let the appeal of what invariably seems to be a sensational story do the rest of the work.[5] The following episode which involved the author serves to illustrate.

The occasion was the Algerian war for independence from France and the efforts of the French Army to suppress the rebellion. As with most such wars, it was bitter, bloody, and prolonged. Most of the Algerians were for independence, although a few collaborated with the French. The colons—native Frenchmen who had settled in Algeria—were bitterly opposed. In continental France opinion was divided, but most wanted to keep Algeria: a matter of pride and prestige. As Charles de Gaulle neared his difficult and courageous decision to give Algeria its independence, a group of generals in the French Army in Algeria revolted and threatened to land paratroopers in Paris and to seize control of the government.

On May 4, 1961, at 6:30 P.M., TASS, the wire service of the Soviet Union, carried the following, dispatched in English, to its European subscribers:

> LONDON—Summing up the results of recent events in Algeria, the *Weekly Tribune* again stresses that the rebels were directly encouraged by the U.S. Central Intelligence Agency and the Kennedy administration. "Stories about CIA personnel being in touch with the rebel generals in Algiers seemed too fantastic to believe when the headlines first broke this weekend," the article says. "However slowly but surely the truth is beginning to emerge. It (several words indistinct) makes spy tales for boys pale into insignificance.
>
> "Point 1—it is indeed true that General Challe was told by CIA that a rebellion in Algeria would be advantageous. By some incredible logic, CIA believed that it might be beneficial to NATO since de Gaulle had been going cool on that organization and Challe had once been deputy head of NATO's European section.
>
> "Point 2—President Kennedy knew the broad outlines of the CIA plan.

[5] See also Ladislav Bittman, *The Deception Game* (Syracuse, N.Y.: Syracuse Research Corp., 1972).

"Point 3—General Challe has spilled the beans to the French government, and relations between France and America have sunk to an all-time low.

"Point 4—It was not a low-level CIA decision. Indeed, Kirkpatrick, deputy only to Allen Dulles, visited Paris to keep informed of events and then flew off to Casablanca on 16 April to see the fireworks from close at hand.

"However the revolt broke out two days before it was planned and fizzled into a giant flop, but not before General Challe had sent a message to President Kennedy asking for both military and financial help which CIA agents had insisted would be sent.

"This put Kennedy on the spot for it was quite obvious to him that the story about CIA involvement would come out. A hasty White House conference was called, and Kennedy then sent a message to de Gaulle offering him aid and including the suggestion that NATO forces might be used to help fight the rebels. In the circumstances, it was about the only thing that Kennedy could do for CIA had landed him in a terrible dilemma. Allen Dulles is going to have a lot more to answer for than just the Cuban failure."

The TASS dispatch was part of the Soviet Union's effort to discredit the United States in the eyes of the French less than a month before President Kennedy was scheduled to make a state visit to France for discussions with President de Gaulle.

This try fell on fertile ground: the atmosphere was receptive. On April 16 Cuban exiles had landed at the Bay of Pigs in the ill-fated attempt to overthrow Castro. President Kennedy acknowledged that the CIA had been responsible for the Cuban operation. On April 22 the French generals staged an abortive mutiny in Algeria. Rumors immediately started to circulate in France that the CIA also had been behind the attempted coup in Algeria.

By May 1 the rumors about CIA involvement had reached such intensity that Allen Dulles, the Director of

Central Intelligence, departed from the usual policy of maintaining strict silence in the face of reports and rumors about CIA and allowed himself to be quoted: "The reports are completely false. The CIA had nothing to do with the rebellion." According to the Washington *Post*, the CIA spokesman, on his own, added that the false reports had been circulated by right-wingers in France.[6]

On May 3, at a luncheon in Paris in honor of the American Ambassador James N. Gavin given by the Anglo-American Press Association, the principal issue was the CIA involvement in Algeria. According to *The New York Times*, ". . . when a British correspondent of the *Evening Standard* of London suggested that the French Foreign Ministry had contributed to the rumor campaign, the Ministry's spokesman, Pierre Baraduc, a luncheon guest, became so incensed that he threatened to leave the room." [7]

Two days later, the French Foreign Minister, Couve de Murville, said: "Contrary to certain insinuations, the French Government had absolutely nothing to do with the growth of these rumors which were spread, further-more, in a much wider context and the French press only reprinted what had been published abroad."

The New York Times dispatch from Paris of May 5, in reporting the statement, provided the following back-ground:

Since the early days of the military putsch of April 22, reports circulated here and were printed first in the Soviet press and then in the French press that "certain members" of "certain American services"—and the Central Intelli-

[6] "Dulles Denies Role in Algiers Rebellion," Washington *Post*, May 2, 1961.
[7] "Gavin's Diplomacy Is Tested in Smoothing a Paris Quarrel," *The New York Times*, May 4, 1961.

gence Agency was clearly the target—had encouraged the rebellious generals.

The *Times* article also said:

> The Minister simply absolved Mr. Kennedy and the United States Government of any blame for possible actions by irresponsible subordinates.
> He did not, however, issue anything like the categorical denial that the United States officials would like to hear from a responsible French source.[8]

To place this rather successful Soviet deception effort in proper perspective, it should be recalled that French pride and honor were involved and that the United States was a logical scapegoat. Just twenty-one years had passed since France's defeat at the hands of the Germans; a defeat that shocked not only the French but the world, when what was reputedly the finest standing army and the most powerful defensive fortification—the Maginot Line—were overwhelmed in just sixty-two days. Four years of occupation followed, in which some 40,000 French patriots in the Resistance were killed by the Germans. Charles de Gaulle, as leader of the Free French, considered himself slighted and ignored by the British and Americans, was not allowed to be present when the first of the liberating forces landed in France in June 1944, and two months later made his way to Paris in order to be there on the day of liberation, against the wishes of his allies.

The United States had urged France to give Indochina independence, but Paris was determined first to reassert authority over the colonies in Southeast Asia. Nine years of frustrating guerrilla warfare were capped by the

---

[8] "French Minister Tries to Halt Rumors of U.S. Role in Mutiny," *The New York Times*, May 6, 1961.

humiliating defeat at Dien Bien Phu. Throughout this period, although America was a NATO ally, France was suspicious of U.S. motives in Indochina. When the United States promptly moved into South Vietnam after the French defeat, these suspicions seemed confirmed.

Then followed the revolt in Algeria—not a colony but under the French Constitution part of France itself. Again, France viewed the American position as ambivalent: supporting France as a keystone in the defense of Western Europe from the Communists, but sympathetic to Algerian independence. President Kennedy had said in a speech in the U.S. Senate in July 1957: "No amount of mutual politeness, wishful thinking, nostalgia or regret should blind either France or the United States to the fact that, if France and the West at large are to have a continuing influence in North Africa . . . the essential first step is the independence of Algeria." [9]

The loss of Indochina was bitter. The decision to liberate Algeria was even harder. When the generals revolted, the hurt deepened. What was more natural than an attempt to blame an organization that had just received worldwide attention attempting to overthrow another government.

The CIA had no role in the Algerian revolt. President Kennedy was a consistent advocate of Algerian independence. The mutinous generals opposed it, and when there appeared a possibility that they might attempt a paratroop attack on Paris, Kennedy promptly promised de Gaulle assistance. As the CIA officer selected by the Russians as a likely "irresponsible subordinate," I was just another target, not necessarily an illogical one. During the Second World War, I had served as an OSS liaison officer to the Free French and had received a Croix de

---

[9] Schlesinger, *A Thousand Days*, p. 553.

Guerre. In 1952 and 1957 I had visited Paris and met with French intelligence and security officials. In 1960 I had been in Paris again, not to meet with the French but as chairman of an intragovernmental committee studying the U.S. foreign intelligence effort. In 1961, as Inspector General of CIA, my name had appeared in the U.S. press on several occasions. And in 1961 not only did I *not* visit either France or Casablanca—in fact, I have never been to Morocco—but on the particular dates mentioned I was in Washington and was almost completely occupied supervising the after-the-event inspection report on the Bay of Pigs disaster.

While the allegations about CIA involvement may have stirred some areas of French public opinion, that in the United States in the spring of 1961 was much more concerned with the Bay of Pigs. The CIA was in grave disrepute. President Kennedy is quoted as saying: ". . . It is a hell of a way to learn things, but I have learned one thing from this business—that is, that we will have to deal with CIA. McNamara has dealt with Defense; Rusk has done a lot with State; but no one has dealt with CIA." [10] The President's obvious displeasure with the CIA led to all sorts of proposals, in the American government and the press, for its reorganization or dismemberment. President Kennedy appointed a special committee to examine what went wrong at the Bay of Pigs; revitalized the Foreign Intelligence Advisory Board; and shortly thereafter appointed a new head of CIA.

As noted earlier, within two years the President's confidence was restored in the CIA and he was willing to record that he regarded it "with esteem."

Only the President and the Congress are in a position to reassure the American people—and thus the world—

[10] *Ibid.*, p. 276.

that the intelligence community is under control. This, however, has been done by the President only in times of crisis—the U-2, the Bay of Pigs, the Diem coup—and the rest of the time the public must have faith. Reports made to the President by his Foreign Intelligence Advisory Board, a body created to advise him on whether the intelligence community is doing its job, are never publicized.

Only very rarely has a President felt compelled to defend the intelligence agencies. After the U-2 was shot down over the Soviet Union in 1960, President Eisenhower acknowledged that he had been aware of the operation, as did President Kennedy a year later about the Bay of Pigs. After the Diem assassination, in November 1963, President Kennedy, in a televised press conference, went even further. There had been considerable press speculation about the activities of the CIA in Vietnam and commentary to the effect that it was out of control. The President told the nationwide audience that he had complete confidence in the agency and regarded it as being under good direction.

Although the congressional committees meet with the CIA several times each session, the hearings are seldom publicized unless the subject happens to be controversial, for example, a difference in the estimate between the CIA and Defense on the missile capabilities of the Soviet Union. There is no periodic report that the subcommittees have reviewed the workings of the intelligence community and found it in order.

On several occasions leaders of the Congress have defended the CIA and the intelligence community in public statements. The powerful Chairman of the House Appropriations Committee, Clarence Cannon, spoke in defense on several occasions, as have Leslie Arends and others. Even Senator J. William Fulbright, a fairly persistent critic of administrations, indicated his confidence in Director Richard Helms.

Some in American society would regard statements on the intelligence community from either the President or the Congress as suspect. If the President declared that the CIA was out of hand, the political reaction would criticize him for losing control. If the Chief Executive announces that he is satisfied, there will be those who will respond as did one former CIA employee who wrote an article entitled "CIA: The President's Obedient Tool." As for Congress, there are those who view the Armed Services Committees as extensions of the military-industrial complex and such reviews undertaken by those bodies as uncritical.

With the rest of the government open to the public view through annual statements and budget hearings, the lack of knowledge about the intelligence community seems even more obvious. As a result, the secrecy, insulation, and isolation of intelligence are increased.

The result is such comments by Lewis Mumford as ". . . secrecy itself became valued as a badge of authority and a method of enforcing control" [11] and:

> . . . the American machine took over the most regressive features of the Czarist-Stalinist system, vastly augmenting both its military force and its agents of centralized control: the Atomic Energy Commission, the Federal Bureau of Investigation, the Central Intelligence Agency, the National Security Agency—all secret agencies whose methods and policies have never been openly discussed or effectively challenged, still less curtailed by the national legislative authority. So deeply entrenched are these agents that they dare to flout and disobey the authority of both the President and the Congress.[12]

[11] *The Pentagon of Power* (New York: Harcourt Brace Jovanovich, 1970), p. 263.

[12] *Ibid.*, p. 266.

Mumford also has this to say:

> In both Russia and the United States, centralized govern-
> mental agencies, unchecked by public opinion, uncontrolled
> by elected bodies, have perfected the technique of the
> "permanent crisis" in order to consolidate the powers that
> were originally designed solely to meet a passing threat.
>
> The Soviet blockade of Berlin was an obvious instance of
> this tendency; but so, equally, was the Central Intelligence
> Agency's provocative continuance of U-2 flights over Russia,
> despite Russian protests, as an effective means of wrecking
> the approaching "Summit Meeting" in Paris in 1960. Con-
> sistently the agents of the megamachine act as if their only
> responsibility were to the power system itself.[13]

These allegations are worth discussing. While to some
the American services may seem to have some Russian
features, the models have been British. It is untrue that
there is a pattern of flouting the President and Congress,
as implied. The record is quite clear to the contrary that
when either the President or Congress felt their wishes
were contravened, changes were made in organization
and leadership. Nor is the allegation that the intelligence
community is "unchecked by public opinion" substan-
tiated. Public opinion, indeed, has been an important if
not decisive factor in the Vietnam War and in the
progressive abandonment of covert political operations.
The claim that the provocative continuance of U-2 flights
was designed to wreck the Summit Meeting is false. The
President was thoroughly aware of the U-2 flights, as
were the Russians, and the Sverdlovsk incident was
Soviet retaliation in embarrassment: they had been
humiliated by the U-2 flights; the United States was to be
humbled by their canceling the Summit.

While one might challenge some of Lewis Mumford's

[13] *Ibid.*, p. 271.

assertions, it is wise to acknowledge that they reflect the concern of many of the intellectuals and liberals in the United States. While most of these abhor secrecy and inherently distrust intelligence and security organizations of any kind, many would acknowledge the necessity to collect and evaluate information. It is the use of the intelligence agencies in political warfare—and to support national policies with which they disagree—that creates the greatest concern.

One scholar who has made a conscientious effort to study the intelligence community and assess its role in American society is Harry Howe Ransom of Vanderbilt University. Ransom says: "Too little serious attention has been given to, and inadequate controls have been exerted over, the intelligence establishment. . . ." [14] He finds congressional review inadequate, urges more external reviews of the intelligence community, and claims that the CIA has taken liberties in interpreting its legally assigned functions.

Other critics add such items as overwhelming military influence, amorality, a cold-war mentality, intrusion into the privacy of individuals. Thus the criticism of the intelligence community is wide, while its support is limited.

Of the agencies in the intelligence community, only the FBI can claim an impressive constituency which will rally to its support. The Society of Former Special Agents of the FBI is not only a fraternal organization of some five thousand members, but a body of loyal alumni. A sizable number of its members are scattered throughout industry in executive and security jobs. An organization known as Americans for Effective Law Enforcement was formed to

[14] *The Intelligence Establishment* (Cambridge, Mass.: Harvard University Press, 1970), p. xiii.

counter the American Civil Liberties Union, and in 1971
Friends of the FBI was created to respond to criticism of
the FBI, especially the Committee for Public Justice.

The CIA has no such organization, although William J.
Donovan, when the OSS was disbanded in 1945, pushed
for the creation of a Veterans of Strategic Services. The
latter never flourished, although most of its membership
would support their former friends and colleagues who
stayed on in the CIA.

The military intelligence agencies can count on strong
support from the veterans' organizations. A National
Counter Intelligence Corps Association is also active.

For the great mass of the American people, intelligence remains a mystery, surfacing occasionally in some
exciting episode of brief duration. Most leave it to the
President to worry about and to control. Perhaps a rough
calculation of public attitude can be made. John Adams
estimated that at the time of the Revolutionary War,
one-third of the colonists were for independence, one-
third loyal to the crown, and one-third apathetic. Perhaps
today a survey would indicate that about a half to
two-thirds of the American people would be able to
identify the CIA or the intelligence community; that
most would consider such organizations necessary but
would have little knowledge of the quality of their work;
that a small percentage would consider them dangerous
or out of control.

7

Intelligence in
a Free Society

Are the intelligence activities of the U.S. government consistent with American ideology? Or has the United States adopted alien techniques—in fact, the methods of its enemies, as some allege—in order to accomplish its objectives? If it has, in fact, done this, then has it succumbed to the philosophy that the ends justify any means? And if the latter is the case, then is American democracy in danger of being destroyed by the means purportedly being used to preserve it?

If the legitimacy of the intelligence community is established, and it has survived a quarter century with each of the major political parties in power for an almost equal portion of that period, then what are the ethical and moral bases for such activities? Perhaps even more important, what are the ethical aspects of intelligence work, and has it served in any way to damage or destroy the morality of the nation?

It would be the height of presumptive arrogance to maintain that any of the views presented in this final chapter represent definitive or conclusive answers to such questions. All that can be expected is that some of the thoughts put forward may shed some light on deep and fundamental problems and lead to more exhaustive study.

The author's views can be summarized rather briefly. While intelligence work may not be among man's most honorable activities, neither is it the least worthy. If the people of the United States believe in their way of life and want it to survive, then they must take the necessary steps for survival. The history of the quarter century following the Second World War seems to provide clear evidence of the contribution made by our intelligence community to the policy-making process. It is, therefore, my contention that we should continue our intelligence efforts until such a state of affairs exists in the world that makes the secret acquisition and handling of information no longer necessary for survival. My views on controls are expressed in the conclusions of Chapter 2: secrecy is no reason why intelligence should not be under just as tight and restrictive controls as the armed forces, diplomacy, commerce, or air traffic—secrecy requires only a nonpublic effort.

In examining intelligence in a "free society" or its relationship to the American "ideology," the most difficult dimensions to establish are: What do we mean by a "free society"? And do we have one? And what are the beliefs that we consider basic to our way of life and do we adhere to them?

One can build the description of our society as it exists by starting with the ultimate and moving to the practical. Obviously, the ultimate is a society in which each person can do exactly as he pleases as long as he does not interfere with others. It is questionable whether man has ever known a totally free society, or ever will. On this planet the growth in population and increase in technology each day tend to be more restrictive of man's freedom: more people with a greater capacity to project their individual activities into areas that affect others. Regardless of what measurements are used, even in the freest of societies, man is faced with ever greater restrictions on his individual or collective activities on the surface of the earth, in the air, on the water, or under it.

A simple analysis of what any person does in the course of a twenty-four-hour period provides convincing proof of fleeting freedoms.

This is an essential background for understanding the American ideology. For nearly four centuries, emigrants have come to America seeking freedom—not absolute freedom, for only the dreamers and the desperate seek that, but relative, compared to the conditions they left. What most have sought was greater freedom to express their political beliefs, to worship their own deities, to develop their well-being in accordance with their ambitions and abilities, to live where and how and with whom they wished. And most wanted to be governed by peers of their own choosing, who could be removed when no longer representative and who would be considered to have governed best if they governed least.

What has perhaps been the most spectacular success of American democracy has been the evolutionary, if frequently delayed, adjustment of the role of the government to maintain the proper relationship between the individual and society. True, on one occasion the adjustment required a great civil war and on many occasions it has required violent protest. It should also be recognized that on no occasion has the consensus on the adjustment required been unanimous, and perhaps on some occasion the changes have been imposed by the minority.

In the area of national security, Americans have been most reluctant or slow to adopt measures that to older nations seemed self-evident or inevitable. Some of this reluctance stemmed from a desire to avoid a growth of government power that might be used to lessen the freedom of the individual. It was with the greatest of hesitation that military forces were authorized even when the threat of war seemed imminent.

After the Revolutionary War, the American Navy

vanished in peacetime; it was not until the British, the French, and the Barbary pirates so disrupted U.S. commerce that the Navy Department was established on April 30, 1798. The American Army, after the Revolution, dropped at one point to eighty-four men, until revived to man the frontier and prepare for threatened wars with England and France. For the next century and a half the Army and Navy shrank during peacetime, to be expanded at emergency pace on the threat of war. A draft for peacetime needs was not instituted until 1948.

Goaded on by extensive British and German propaganda efforts in the First World War, the United States established a Committee on Public Information on April 14, 1917, to inform the American public about the war effort and to win friends abroad. This was disbanded on June 20, 1919. An Office of the Coordinator of Information (COI) was established in 1940 combining propaganda and intelligence—in fact, many elements of irregular and psychological warfare. In 1942 COI was split into the Office of Strategic Services and the Office of War Information, the latter created to inform the world about the American war effort. It was not until 1948 that the use of public media to support national objectives abroad in peacetime was authorized by P.L. 480, the United States Information and Educational Exchange Act. This set up the International Information Administration, which under the Reorganization Act of 1953 became the United States Information Agency. But even then, congressional concern that such an organization might be used to propagandize the American people, or for political purposes, put the forces of USIA abroad—not in the United States.

The evolution of the intelligence community, the most modern of the mechanisms of government for national security, has been detailed in the previous pages.

What, then, has been the effect of this creation of a formidable peacetime intelligence establishment on the freedoms of the nation?

If one is to believe some of what has been written about the intelligence community and the CIA in particular, we are in grave peril of being subverted by a portion of the government created to protect our national security. If the difference between the means used to accomplish national objectives is the primary distinction between a free society and an authoritarian state, then perhaps we have already sown the seeds which will destroy our freedoms.

In a democracy there is a constant evaluation process as to what means are acceptable in the pursuit of national objectives, and success alone is not always a valid criterion. In a totalitarian society any means that are successful are valid.

In Iran, Guatemala, and Cuba, the United States attempted to use covert operations to accomplish foreign policy objectives; note that in all three instances the effort was approved at the highest level of the government. In two cases the effort was successful, but the hand of the United States was soon known. At the Bay of Pigs, where U.S. involvement was immediately known, the failure was of such magnitude as to result in the adoption of a national policy severely limiting all such types of activities in the future. In fact, it can be argued that a successful covert political operation can only be one that is never known, although the counterargument is that if an operation blocks a Communist takeover it has furthered the objectives of U.S. policy.

Americans generally express the ideal that no nation should interfere in the internal affairs of another, and thus covert operations appear to be a particularly flagrant method of interference, perhaps because of the secrecy involved and the possibility that such operations are common practice. Thus the means of a covert operation seem even more offensive than the use of armed force, economic pressure, or political manipulation, all of which can be seen and accounted for.

Two deep-rooted fears are behind the concern about covert operations. The first is reflected in the oft-repeated allegation that the CIA is uncontrolled and uncontrollable; that it makes policy, determines the course of action, and then does what is necessary. Those advancing this charge cite a broad range of presumptive evidence: by virtue of some decades of experience, the CIA now has acquired a clandestine mentality and instinctively turns to the covert to accomplish national objectives; dominant military influence in the intelligence community always prescribes taking action; the way of life imposed by the secrecy requirements of the intelligence community goes so far as to hide activities from the view of the responsible elected officials and policy-makers; intelligence personnel do not believe that the government is sufficiently determined and thus take matters into their own hands; this is truly "the invisible government," the secret state within the state. Some voicing such views cite the experiences of Nazi Germany and the Soviet Union, in which intelligence and security agencies became too powerful and were used to destroy freedoms.

These fears reflect concern about what goes on behind the closed doors of the intelligence agencies, those marked "authorized persons only," and worry over what might be said in papers marked "Top Secret" and "Eyes Only." If the concern is over what is unknown, there is enough known to reinforce the fear. The Watergate incident of 1972, when former FBI and CIA personnel were caught in the Democratic party headquarters, seemed to reflect the clandestine mentality and the tendency to take matters in their own hands. How was the public to know that this was not representative of the attitude of the intelligence and security organizations toward American institutions?

However, such critics tend to discount the effectiveness of congressional review and to ignore the fact that the committees are quick to investigate any evidence of the misuse of authority in the executive branches of the government.[1] In effect, such critics are implying that all U.S. government personnel, civilian or military, are amoral, for only if that were the case could such abuse of power take place: there being such divergencies of views both within agencies and between departments that it would be difficult for arbitrary, illegal, or unilateral action to go unnoticed or unchallenged. Anyone assuming that a covert operation could be mounted in any country without the U.S. ambassador and his embassy being aware is both unjustly impugning the ability of the Foreign Service and the responsibility of the intelligence personnel who are required to keep the chief-of-mission informed of their activities. Finally, there is fear the President would use the intelligence services for unauthorized activities.

The President has his own staff, the Office of Management and Budget and the Foreign Intelligence Advisory Board, to watch for abuse of authority both at home and abroad. Further, chief executives generally are sensitive to congressional and public criticism. Three recent

[1] For example, the grand jury and congressional investigations of the Watergate incident and Senator Ervin's previous extensive investigation of the Army's surveillance of citizens in the United States; the Senate Foreign Relations Committee's frequent reviews of activities in Vietnam; the study of the PHOENIX operation (to eliminate the Vietcong infrastructure in Vietnam) by the House Government Operations and Information subcommittees. One should not forget the General Accounting Office, a vehicle of Congress, as an effective watchdog.

illustrations of Presidential sensitivity to intelligence weaknesses are pertinent. In 1956 President Eisenhower personally reviewed intelligence operations in Berlin after the Russians protested, but discovered it was a case of the fox complaining about the chickens. After the Bay of Pigs in 1961, President Kennedy had a special committee investigate the operation and changed the leadership of the CIA. President Nixon in 1971 directed a review of intelligence procedures and gave the Director of Central Intelligence greater authority after the White House staff pointed out intelligence weaknesses. He followed this in 1973 with the naming of a new Director of Central Intelligence who was instructed to reduce the size of the intelligence community, eliminate duplication, and make reforms in the national estimates system.

The second fear about covert operations is that the President will use secret means to implement unpopular policies. In the Vietnam War period, this was a persistent criticism, inasmuch as the intelligence agencies obviously were very much involved in the war effort.

The PHOENIX operation is a case in point. Initiated by the CIA in 1967 and later taken over by the Army, its mission was to discover and remove from the civilian population of South Vietnam the so-called enemy infrastructure, the political leaders and the agents of the Vietcong. Over the years the inevitable statistics were produced on the number of VC who were persuaded to defect, or who were captured or killed, and the operation acquired an unsavory reputation as an assassination program. While the effort might be described as an effort at "Vietnamization," the question could be asked whether it was either wise or productive in a limited war and whether the terror tactics employed by the South Vietnamese mercenaries did not alienate even more people from loyalty to the Saigon government.

Perhaps it would not be remiss to point out that the Congress of the United States, the elected representatives of the people, had within its power the ability to stop all American action in Vietnam, including intelligence operations, but never did. It could be assumed that if the Congress believed that the President was using the intelligence agencies for other than the national interest, there would be an immediate outcry, especially when many within the President's own party were critical of the Vietnam War. Such did not happen.

The publication of the Pentagon Papers did much to ease the fears of responsible critics that the CIA and the intelligence agencies were submissive and servile, tailoring intelligence estimates to policy needs. The evidence that these documents provide is reassurance that the intelligence community attempts to be dispassionate and objective, presenting the prospects as bleakly as the available facts may require despite the obvious hope at the highest level for more encouraging opinions. The fact that the decision-makers overrode, or ignored, or considered the intelligence estimates just another opinion may well provide those who govern the nation in the future with the incentive to give due weight to the intelligence estimates.

The suggestion has been made that the Congress be provided with National Intelligence Estimates. In July 1971 Senator John Sherman Cooper introduced a resolution that would require the CIA to provide the Foreign Relations and Armed Services Committees in both houses with the same evaluations and analyses it gives to the White House. At hearings held on the resolution in March 1972, two former senior officials of the CIA, Chester Cooper and Herbert Scoville, testified in favor of the proposal. If the Congress receives the same material as the President, the issue then becomes what policy should be followed, and one can foresee intense differences between the executive and the legislature. On the other hand, it would provide continual check for the Congress and force closer cooperation by the executive branch. The President is unlikely to volunteer such information, claiming that the conduct of foreign relations is his. Should the Congress enact legislation requiring the submission of intelligence reports, a question of constitutionality may arise. There is no doubt that the receipt of such reports would give the Congress a much more powerful voice in the formulation and implementation of foreign policy.

Fears about covert operations abroad relate directly to concern about intelligence activities in the United States. If the CIA can overthrow the governments of other nations, could it do the same here?

The iceberg analogy is frequently used and is appropriate in discussing the activities of the intelligence community in the United States. If periodic exposures of the intelligence agencies at work domestically are indicative, cannot it be assumed that there is a vast amount under the surface that is not seen? Anybody who has viewed the skepticism in a university lecture hall when told there are no federal agents on the campus, that antiwar protestors are not under surveillance unless suspected of subversion or criminal activity, that "Big Brother" is not watching them would know what I mean.

The publication of the "Media Papers," those stolen from the FBI files in Pennsylvania, reinforced the fears about a police state. If the FBI wanted sources on all college and university campuses, what was the reason? Did the bureau believe that students and/or faculty actually were conspiring to overthrow the government of the United States? Was there evidence of alien agents on the campuses that posed a threat to the internal security of the nation? Were the universities assumed to be producing graduates who would devote their lives to subversion of our institutions? Was the authority for such activity specifically from the Attorney General or the President? And, if so, was it reflective of a general concern about the safety of the nation or of irritation at opposition to administration policies?

Militating against trust and confidence in the intelligence community have been such episodes as the use of the National Student Association and private foundations by the CIA; Michigan State University contracting for police training in Vietnam; the Army's CAMELOT operation using a university to study potential revolutionaries in foreign countries; the assembling by the Pentagon of information on potential troublemakers in the cities; the CIA's attempts to have books suppressed or changed.[2] Fears that such operations continue or even multiply persist despite President Johnson's directive to the contrary.

The heart of the matter is that the American people will tolerate what must be done to protect the nation as long as it does not seem to destroy what it is protecting.

The CIA is expected to know what is going on in the world and is heartily criticized if it doesn't. The CIA is viewed with suspicion when used as an instrument of political warfare and with alarm when it uses private institutions to cover its activities.

---

[2] In my opinion, the CIA has a valid and legal right to require all former employees to submit books and articles on intelligence matters for review prior to publication to insure that no security breaches have been committed. This requirement of the CIA, which every employee agrees to in writing before being employed by the agency, has been upheld by the U.S. Fourth Circuit Court of Appeals. Where the CIA has attempted to persuade those who have never worked in intelligence to change books, it has usually been unavailing and led to publicity (probably selling more books), which persuades people that the CIA is trying to restrict the freedom of the press.

If the FBI did not apprehend spies and saboteurs and give clear evidence of its attention to the activities of foreign nations in the United States, it would be subject to severe criticism. But decades of witch hunts have convinced many that we are following the path toward a totalitarian state and that hordes of federal investigators are invading the privacy of millions.

The military services are expected to defend the nation and fight successful wars. The Constitution also says that the Army will be used to suppress civil disorders, but happily this has been required quite rarely. The necessity to use the Army in the cities in the late sixties, and the subsequent revelation that the military gathered vast quantities of information on potential troublemakers, served to strengthen worries about a garrison state. These worries should not be ignored or dismissed as the mouthings of liberals or radicals who are against everything the government does. It would be a mistake to dismiss all academics as anarchists, for certainly a majority in the universities accept the necessity for intelligence and security services, if kept within appropriate bounds. Nor should such criticism be regarded as an unhappy by-product of the Vietnam War that will cease when that conflict ends.

The criticism of our institutions is as fundamental a right as we have in the American system guaranteed by the freedoms of the press, speech, and assembly. The intelligence community should have no immunity. If their errors become public knowledge, the incentive must be toward greater professionalism, not suppression of the news. In the quarters where action can be taken—the White House and Congress—irresponsible criticism is quickly discounted, while the valid critiques can result in corrective measures.

Undoubtedly, the necessity for secrecy can become

obsessive. No rational critic would argue for the publication of classified information of value to forces hostile to the United States or dedicated to the destruction of its way of life. On the other hand, a constant effort for a minimum amount of secrecy—occasional official release of nonsensitive information about the work of the intelligence community—would help to alleviate the fear of the secret and powerful system. The recent appearance of CIA-produced reports on the publication list of the Government Printing Office, available for public purchase, is a step in the right direction. Sanitization and declassification of CIA research reports for use by scholars would do much to break down the mutual barriers of hostility that now exist.

Much of the responsibility for establishing public confidence and trust in the intelligence community rests with the President and the Congress. The occasional reassurance forthcoming from the White House and Capitol Hill is not sufficient. There should be periodic reports from both branches.

The President's Foreign Intelligence Advisory Board is required to report twice a year. On such occasions, a brief statement from the White House, as frank as possible within the bounds of security, would be a reminder to the citizenry that men of responsibility and stature had reviewed the work of the intelligence community.

Equally important, the Armed Services and Appropriations Committees, at least once in each session, should report to the Congress that they have reviewed the budgets and work of the intelligence agencies and taken the necessary action. One could also hope that the parent committees might see fit to hold question periods in executive session at which the other members of the Congress could raise matters of concern to them and be told the facts. The argument against this is that the standing committees do not wish to share their information and power and worry about leaks, but parochial jealousy should not stand in the way of national interest.

Until the Congress and the White House issue fuller and franker reports about such matters as the state of affairs in the intelligence community, we will continue to have enlightenment by leak: secret documents passed to newsmen; conscience-salving recriminations by those with afterthoughts about policies; money-making revelations by alleged insiders. It is a sad commentary that many Americans are convinced that the only way they will ever learn what is going on in the government is by leaks and from defectors. The modern American tragedy is that many citizens have lost their confidence in the truthfulness of their government officials.

And therein rests the crux of the issue of intelligence in a free society: confidence in the men responsible for secret operations. By its very nature such work, in the popular image, would seem to require a person with special characteristics: secretive, superpatriotic, conspiratorial, devious, deceptive—in sum, dangerous. To say that this is not so and that for secretive you substitute careful, for superpatriotic, disciplined, for conspiratorial, meticulous, for devious, subtle, for deceptive, unobtrusive, and for dangerous, dependable, is not convincing. The image is there and must be changed.

The New York Times writers, in their series on the CIA, came to the conclusion after five articles and some thirty thousand words that the problem of controlling the CIA must begin with the men inside the organization and that the "qualities of the director (are) viewed as chief rein on the agency." [3]

---

[3] *The New York Times*, April 29, 1966.

The directors of the intelligence community are public officials even though their employees may be invisible. The Director of Central Intelligence and his deputy and the Director of the FBI are appointed by the President with the advice and consent of the Senate. The Congress also has a voice in the rank and assignment of military officers. Thus the appointment and review of the key men in intelligence rests with the representatives of the people.

But it goes beyond just having faith in the directors of the intelligence and security organizations. The people in a free society must have faith in the institutions as well: not blind faith, but educated and informed confidence built up over years of trustworthy and effective performance.

How can this be accomplished when public confidence in the government is badly shaken over My Lai, over PHOENIX, over Watergate—to mention only the three most obvious symbols? It must be done by that democratic process that has served the United States so well for two centuries: recurrent, exhaustive scrutiny by respected critics, followed by the purging of policies and practices found to be repugnant to American ideals. This must be done by the President and by the Congress, if necessary under the pressure of public opinion. The secrecy requirements of the intelligence community do not prevent such inquiries. There have been several extensive and valuable reviews of the system which resulted in important changes. These must continue, and the public should be made aware of the effort. Confidence will be restored by such action and by the evidence of the results. The intelligence community is sufficiently visible in our free society to demonstrate its effectiveness and integrity.

THE WHITE HOUSE

January 16, 1962

MEMORANDUM FOR: Director of Central Intelligence

In carrying out your newly assigned duties as Director of Central Intelligence it is my wish that you serve as the Government's principal foreign intelligence officer, and as such that you undertake, as an integral part of your responsibility, the coordination and effective guidance of the total United States foreign intelligence effort. As the Government's principal intelligence officer, you will assure the proper coordination, correlation, and evaluation of intelligence from all sources and its prompt dissemination to me and to other recipients as appropriate. In fulfillment of these tasks I shall expect you to work closely with the heads of all departments and agencies having responsibilities in the foreign intelligence field.

In coordinating and guiding the total intelligence effort, you will serve as Chairman of the United States Intelligence Board, with a view to assuring the efficient and effective operation of the Board and its associated bodies. In this connection I note with approval that you have designated your deputy to serve as a member of the Board, thereby bringing to the Board's deliberations the relevant facts and judgments of the Central Intelligence Agency.

As directed by the President and the National Security Council, you will establish with the advice and assistance of the United States Intelligence Board the necessary policies and procedures to assure adequate coordination of foreign intelligence activities at all levels.

With the heads of the Departments and Agencies concerned you will maintain a continuing review of the programs and activities of all U.S. agencies engaged in foreign intelligence activities with a view to assuring efficiency and effectiveness and to avoiding undesirable duplication.

As head of the Central Intelligence Agency, while you will continue to have over-all responsibility for the Agency, I shall expect you to delegate to your principal deputy, as you may deem necessary, so much of the direction of the detailed operation of the Agency as may be required to permit you to carry out your primary task as Director of Central Intelligence.

It is my wish that you keep me advised from time to time as to your progress in the implementation of this directive and as to any recommendations you may have which would facilitate the accomplishment of these objectives.

JOHN F. KENNEDY

cc: Secretary of State
     Secretary of Defense
     Attorney General
     Chairman, Atomic Energy Commission

For Further Reading

A number of books have been written about intelligence in general and espionage or covert operations in particular. The number of articles in newspapers and periodicals also is large, each foreign policy failure or exposed intelligence operation (actual or alleged) setting off a spate of so-called inside stories.

The volume of worthwhile material on intelligence is quite limited. This selective bibliography lists, with appropriate comments, those books and articles worthy of attention, but also includes some of the less accurate but more sensational exposures.

INTELLIGENCE: GENERAL

Strategic Intelligence for American World Policy, by Sherman Kent, Princeton, N.J.: Princeton University Press, 1949, 1966. One of the most scholarly of the books on intelligence by a man who followed the original publication of this book with a career of a quarter-century in the CIA in charge of the production of National Intelligence Estimates.

Strategic Intelligence Production, by Washington Platt, New York: Praeger, 1957. Some valuable descriptions of intelligence production with an analysis of probability and forecasting. The author served in both military intelligence and the CIA and his comments on the intelligence profession are based on experience.

The Future of American Secret Intelligence, by George S. Pettee, Washington: Infantry Journal Press, 1946. A pre-CIA discussion of the need for a first-class intelligence service based rather heavily on the Second World War experience.

The Craft of Intelligence, by Allen W. Dulles, New York: Harper & Row, 1963. An analysis of the intelligence profession by this CIA Director (1953–61) who also was a very successful intelligence officer in Switzerland in the Second World War. He does not deal to any great extent with clandestine techniques.

The Spy in America, by George S. Bryan, Philadelphia: Lippincott, 1943. The history of American intelligence from the Revolutionary War until the end of the First World War.

Turncoats, Traitors and Heroes, by John Bakeless, Philadelphia: Lippincott, 1959. The best account of espionage in the American Revolution.

THE INTELLIGENCE COMMUNITY

The Invisible Government, by David Wise and Thomas B. Ross, New York: Random House, 1964. This book · created a considerable stir when first published with its thesis of secret manipulations hidden in the bowels of the government plotting the subversion of the world behind the President's back. It contains many inaccuracies.

Central Intelligence and National Security, by Harry Howe Ransom, Cambridge, Mass.: Harvard University Press, 1958. An early account of the U.S. intelligence community.

The Intelligence Establishment, by Harry Howe Ransom, Cambridge, Mass.: Harvard University Press, 1970. A revision and expansion of an earlier book, this is an earnest appraisal of how the intelligence community looks from the outside. As a balanced and scholarly discussion it deserves serious consideration.

THE CIA

The Real CIA, Lyman B. Kirkpatrick, Jr., New York: Macmillan, 1968. Autobiographical in part, this book describes in some detail the origins and history of CIA through the

McCone directorship to 1965. Of particular interest are the chapters on the Bay of Pigs, the Joint Study Group, the McCone reorganization, and the role of the Director of Central Intelligence.

The Central Intelligence Agency: Problem of Secrecy in a Democracy, edited with an introduction by Young Hum Kim, Lexington, Mass.: D. C. Heath, 1968. A compilation of twelve articles on the CIA rather heavily weighted toward those "viewing-with-alarm."

The Senator Gravel Edition–The Pentagon Papers, edited by Mike Gravel, Boston: Beacon Press, 1971, Volumes I-IV; Critical Essays and an Index to Volumes I-IV, Noam Chomsky and Howard Zinn, eds. There are more intelligence directives and national estimates in these volumes than in any other public source.

The New York Times (a five-article series on the CIA):

Monday, April 25, 1966, "CIA: Maker of Policy, or Tool?"

Tuesday, April 26, 1966, "How CIA Put 'Instant Air Force' into Congo"

Wednesday, April 27, 1966, "CIA Spies From 100 Miles Up; Satellite Probes Secrets of Soviet"

Thursday, April 28, 1966, "CIA Operations: A Plot Scuttled"

Friday, April 29, 1966, "The CIA: Qualities of Director Viewed as Chief Rein on Agency"

An objective and well-balanced analysis of the CIA's successes and failures based on extensive research and numerous interviews and written by the *Times* top team of national reporters. Contrary to expectations, the *Times* concluded by giving the CIA good marks.

THE FBI AND INTERNAL SECURITY

The Federal Investigators, by Miriam Ottenberg, Englewood Cliffs, N.J.: Prentice-Hall, 1962. An analysis of the investigative agencies of the government, still valuable despite the passage of time.

The FBI Story: A Report to the People, by Don Whitehead, New York: Random House, 1956. A favorable view.

The FBI Nobody Knows, by Fred J. Cook, New York: Macmillan, 1964. A hostile view.

The Federal Bureau of Investigation, by Max Lowenthal, New
   York: William Sloane Associates, 1950. A critical analysis of
   the history of the FBI from its origin through the 1940's.

The Codebreakers: The Story of Secret Writing, by David Kahn,
   New York: Macmillan, 1967. While one might disagree with
   the opening sentence of the preface, "Codebreaking is the
   most important form of secret intelligence in the world
   today," this nevertheless remains the most authoritative book
   on communications intelligence.
The American Black Chamber, by Herbert O. Yardley, Indianapolis: Bobbs-Merrill, 1931. *The* classic on the origins of the
   U.S. communications intelligence effort.

The Game of Nations: The Amorality of Power Politics, by
   Miles Copeland, New York: College Notes and Textbooks,
   1969. The occasionally not-so-covert aspects of political
   warfare on the international scale.
A Short Course in the Secret War, by Christopher Felix
   (pseudo.), New York: Dutton, 1963. Some valuable insights
   by a former "operator."
The Deception Game, by Ladislav Bittman, Syracuse, N.Y.:
   Syracuse Research Corp., 1972. A description of Soviet and
   Czech deception activities.

Secret Missions: The Story of an Intelligence Officer, Captain
   Ellis M. Zacharias, New York: Putnam, 1946. The interesting
   memoirs of a naval intelligence officer.
Captains without Eyes: Intelligence Failures in World War II,
   by Lyman B. Kirkpatrick, Jr., New York: Macmillan, 1969.
   Why intelligence failed in five battles: the Axis attacks on
   Russia, Pearl Harbor, Dieppe, Arnhem, and the Ardennes.
G-2, Intelligence for Patton, by Oscar W. Koch and Robert G.

Hays, Philadelphia: Whitemore, 1971. General Patton's outstanding intelligence chief in the Second World War describes the workings of combat intelligence.

"CONUS Intelligence: The Army Watches Civilian Politics,"
by Christopher Pyle, *Washington Monthly*, January 1970.
The source of the controversy over the Army's collection of
information on civilians.

The Military Attaché, by Alfred Vagts, Princeton, N.J.: Princeton University Press, 1967. An excellent account of the development of the attaché system.

Pearl Harbor, Warning and Decision, by Roberta Wohlstetter,
Stanford, Calif.: Stanford University Press, 1962. The best
case study of why the Japanese achieved surprise on December 7, 1941.

OVERHEAD RECONNAISSANCE

Air Spy: The Story of Photo Intelligence in World War II, by
Constance Babington-Smith, New York: Harper & Row,
1957. A British photo-interpreter details the development of
aerial reconnaissance in the Second World War.

Secret Sentries in Space, by Philip J. Klass, New York: Random
House, 1971. An authoritative account of space satellites.

THE OFFICE OF STRATEGIC SERVICES

Cloak and Dagger: The Secret Story of OSS, by Lt. Col. Corey
Ford and Maj. Alastair MacBain, New York: Random House,
1945. Put together quickly after the end of the war, a series
of episodes from OSS files with an emphasis on paramilitary
operations.

Sub Rosa: The OSS and American Espionage, by Stewart Alsop
and Thomas Braden, New York: Harcourt Brace Jovanovich,
1964. Originally written in 1946 with a new edition in 1964,
to which was added a commentary on the CIA.

You're Stepping on My Cloak and Dagger, by Roger Hall, New
York: W. W. Norton, 1967. A humorous autobiography of an
OSS officer, but also a vivid presentation of the work of the
wartime agency.

The O.S.S. and I, by William J. Morgan, New York: Norton, 1957. A more serious approach by an OSS officer who was first on the training staff and later an operator behind German lines in France.

Donovan of O.S.S., by Corey Ford, Boston: Little, Brown, 1970. While primarily a biography of Donovan, this is the best work on the OSS by one of the authors of *Cloak and Dagger,* himself an OSS veteran.

OSS: The Secret History of America's First Central Intelligence Agency, by R. Harris Smith, Berkeley, Calif.: University of California Press, 1972. Based to a large degree on interviews with OSS veterans, with attention to the books and articles, a good effort in the absence of access to the official files.

The Secret Surrender, by Allen W. Dulles, New York: Harper & Row, 1963. The story of how the author, then the OSS chief in Switzerland, succeeded in negotiating an early surrender of the Germans in Italy.

Assessment of Men, U.S. Office of Strategic Services, Psychological Assessment Staff, New York: Rinehart, 1948. A most valuable contribution to personnel evaluations made by the staff that studied the qualities of the OSS personnel who operated behind enemy lines.

The Scarlet Thread: Adventures in Wartime Espionage, by Donald Downes, London: Derek Versholye, 1953. The history of an OSS officer's activities in Italy in the Second World War.

Behind the Burma Road: The Story of America's Most Successful Guerrilla Force, by William R. Peers and Dean Brelis, Boston: Little, Brown, 1963. A fascinating history of Detachment 101 of the OSS, which operated behind the Japanese lines in Burma, as told by its commander and one of his officers.

OTHER INTELLIGENCE SERVICES

The Russians:

Soviet Espionage, by David J. Dallin, New Haven: Yale University Press, 1955. A comprehensive study for the period 1917–50.

Handbook of Intelligence and Guerrilla Warfare, by Alexander Orlov, Ann Arbor, Mich.: University of Michigan Press, 1963. An authoritative description of Soviet methods by an ex-NKVD officer.

The Great Terror, by Robert Conquest, New York: Macmillan, 1968. The best account of Soviet intelligence and security services during Stalin's purges.

The Case of Richard Sorge, by F. W. Deakin and G. R. Storry, New York: Harper & Row, 1966. A well-researched analysis of the Soviet espionage net in Japan in the Second World War.

Handbook for Spies, by Alexander Foote, Garden City, N.Y.: Doubleday, 1949. An account of Soviet espionage in Switzerland in the Second World War by one of the operators.

Codeword: Direktor, by Heinz Hohne, New York: Coward, McCann and Geoghegan, 1971. An excellent account of the battle between the Soviet and German services in the Second World War.

Strangers on a Bridge, by James B. Donovan, New York: Popular Library, 1964. An interesting analysis of convicted Soviet agent Rudolf Abel by his defense counsel.

The Philby Conspiracy, by Bruce Page, David Leitch, and Phillip Knightley, Garden City, N.Y.: Doubleday, 1968. The best study of the work of Soviet agents Philby, Burgess, and MacLean in the British government.

My Secret War, by Kim Philby, New York: Dell, 1968. This should be read after the Page, Leitch, Knightley book, with the understanding that Philby wrote it in Moscow under the direction and guidance of the Soviet intelligence service and that it is an effort at psychological warfare.

Report of the Royal Commission on Espionage, Commonwealth of Australia, Sydney: A. H. Pettifer, 1955. A valuable report on Soviet activities in Australia.

Empire of Fear, by Vladimir and Evdokia Petrov, New York: Praeger, 1956. The head of Soviet espionage in Australia, and a long-time career officer, writes his autobiography.

The Secret World, by Peter Deriabin and Frank Gibney, Garden City, N.Y.: Doubleday, 1959. A former KGB officer's memoir of the Soviet intelligence and security services.

An Agent in Place: The Wennerstrom Affair, by Thomas Whiteside, New York: Viking Press, 1966. The story of a Swedish officer who worked for the Soviets.

Inside a Soviet Embassy, by Aleksandr Kaznacheev, Philadelphia: Lippincott, 1962. A description of the intelligence activities mounted from the Soviet mission in Burma.

The British:

Intelligence at the Top: The Recollections of an Intelligence Officer, by Sir Kenneth Strong, Garden City, N.Y.: Doubleday, 1969. The G-2 of General Eisenhower's staff in Europe in the Second World War describes the British system.

Room 3603, by H. Montgomery Hyde, New York: Farrar, Straus & Giroux, 1963. A description of the British intelligence center in New York in the Second World War, and its work with the FBI and the OSS.

The Double-Cross System in the War of 1939–1945, by Sir John C. Masterman, New Haven, Conn.: Yale University Press, 1972. This is the authoritative description of how the British gained control of the German intelligence agents in England and used them to deceive the Nazis about the landing in Normandy.

The Man Who Never Was, by Ewen Montague, Philadelphia: Lippincott, 1954. The story of a classic deception operation.

The French:

Lamia, by P. L. Thyraud de Vosjoli, Boston: Little, Brown, 1970. The memoirs of a career officer in the French intelligence service whose last assignment was in Washington.

Ten Thousand Eyes, by Richard Collier, New York: Dutton, 1958. The intelligence activities of the French Resistance against the Germans in the Second World War.

The Unknown Warriors: A Personal Account of the French Resistance, by Guillain de Benouville, New York: Simon and Schuster, 1949. One of the best accounts of a massive national effort.

Souvenirs, by Andre Dewavrin, Cannes: L'Imprinerie Robandy, 1947, 1948, 1951. The memoirs of the chief of de Gaulle's intelligence service in London, in three volumes.

The Germans:

The Service: The Memoirs of General Reinhard Gehlen, New

York: World Publishing, 1972. The head of German military intelligence on the Russian front in the Second World War, and thereafter of the West German service, states his case.

The General Was a Spy, by Heinz Hohne and Hermann Zolling, New York: Coward, McCann and Geoghegan, 1971. A journalistic account of General Gehlen's career.

The Chinese:

Chinese Communist Judiciary, Police and Secret Service, by Asian Peoples Anti-Communist League, Taipei: APACL, 1958. This has been somewhat dated by changes in the CPR.

The Israelis:

The Shattered Silence: The Eli Cohen Affair, by Zwi Aldouby and Jerrold Ballinger, New York: Coward, McCann and Geoghegan, 1971. The fascinating account of a master spy in one of the world's most effective intelligence services.

Diary of the Sinai Campaign, by Moshe Dayan, New York: Harper and Row, 1966. Some interesting contrasts are shown in the quality of intelligence gotten and used by the belligerents.

Index